The Baptist Confession of Faith 1689

or, The Second London Confession
with Scripture Proofs

from the edition of C. H. Spurgeon, 1855

Updated with notes by Peter Masters

The Wakeman Trust, London

THE BAPTIST CONFESSION OF FAITH 1689

©1981 This edited text and notes by Peter Masters
First published 1981 in magazine format
Reprinted 1982, 1984, 1987
Paperback edition 1989
This edition 1998
Reprinted 2006, 2008

THE WAKEMAN TRUST
(Wakeman Trust is a UK Registered Charity)

UK Registered Office
38 Walcot Square
London SE11 4TZ

USA Office
300 Artino Drive
Oberlin, OH 44074-1263
Website: www.wakemantrust.org

ISBN 978 1 870855 24 2

Cover design by Andrew Sides

Printed by BookMasters, Inc., Ashland, Ohio, USA.

Preface by C. H. Spurgeon

[In 1855 a reprinting of the Baptist Confession was issued by C. H. Spurgeon, primarily for the members of his own congregation. Spurgeon's words of introduction perfectly express the great value of this magnificent statement of doctrine.]

'This ancient document is a most excellent epitome of the things most surely believed among us. By the preserving hand of the Triune Jehovah we have been kept faithful to the great points of our glorious Gospel, and we feel more resolved perpetually to abide by them.

'This little volume is not issued as an authoritative rule, or code of faith, whereby ye are to be fettered, but as an assistance to you in controversy, a confirmation in faith, and a means of edification in righteousness. Here the younger members of our church will have a body of divinity in small compass, and by means of the scriptural proofs, will be ready to give a reason for the hope that is in them.

'Be not ashamed of your faith; remember it is the ancient Gospel of martyrs, confessors, reformers, and saints. Above all, it is the *Truth of God* against which the gates of hell cannot prevail. Let your lives adorn your faith, let your example recommend your creed. Above all, live in Christ Jesus, and walk in Him, giving credence to no teaching but that which is manifestly approved of Him, and owned by the Holy Spirit. Cleave fast to the Word of God, which is here mapped out to you.'

Introduction to this Updated Edition

In this edition the *Confession* has been updated so that archaic, antiquated words (and word endings) have been replaced with their modern equivalents. The punctuation has also been updated, and difficult-to-follow sentences have been reconstructed, but as little as possible to ensure faithful reproduction of the original sense. Where further explanation was felt to be necessary, or where much more modern words were called for, these have been inserted additionally in italic brackets.

There are therefore two stages of revision represented in this edition: the gentle, minimal updating of the basic text, and the larger alterations which are clearly shown as extra material. By this two-stage method the original *Confession* has been preserved to keep its meaning in every detail.

To modernise the *Confession* too much introduces two very serious problems. One arises from the extremely tight, precise wording of the *Confession*. To rewrite its sentences in modern English without losing many of the finer points and implications is virtually impossible, unless they are rewritten at two or three times the original length.

The second problem arises from the flowing nature of modern English prose, which is not really suited to the *Confession*. As with modern paraphrases of the Bible, the reader is swept through deep and profound statements without even realising it. The mind barely registers the weighty significance of each phrase. In this respect the rather legal cast of seventeenth-century English is more helpful, for it focuses attention on each phrase in turn (like the more conservative Bible translations). For this reason this edition keeps very closely to the rhythm and mould of the original, assisting some of the long sentences by breaking them up (with artificial paragraph indentations) so as to emphasise the separate points.

The reader may feel inclined to disagree with some of the bracketed synonyms. It seems fairly clear that a number of words in the original *Confession* had a meaning (in the seventeenth century) which was closer to their Latin word source. Where there is evidence for this, the synonym has been chosen to represent the sense probably intended by the compilers of the *Confession*. As an exceptional case, chapter 20 paragraph 3 is included in its original form with a reconstructed version following. This is because that paragraph is rather ambiguous, and required more clarification than was normal.

It is hoped that this revision will provide a text close enough to the original to serve as a faithful edition of it in the legal sense, and yet be sufficiently updated to help another generation of users to discover the riches it contains.

Origin of the 1689 Confession

The first confession of faith to be issued by Particular Baptists appeared in 1644, before the appearance of the *Westminster Confession*. It emphasised the immersion of properly-dressed people and distinguished Particular Baptists from General Baptists by including articles on election, particular redemption, the fallen state of man's will, and the perseverance of the saints. Known as the *London Confession* it was revised in 1651 (with statements designed to counter the Quaker 'inner-light' method of interpreting Scripture, a teaching which has returned again in the 'higher-life' movement).

In 1643 the Long Parliament (having abolished the hierarchy of the Church of England) called the Westminster Assembly of Divines to draw up the government, worship and doctrines of the church. That assembly of outstanding Puritans began to work on their *Confession of Faith* at the beginning of 1645, sixty to eighty divines attending the sessions.

The *Confession* took one year to complete, but was referred back to the compilers by Parliament so that marginal notes could be added 'to prove every point of it with Scripture.' This was completed in April 1647.

The Congregationalists (at the Savoy Conference, 1658) took the *Westminster Confession* as their basis of faith after making modifications.

Then, in 1677, the Particular Baptists also took the *Westminster Confession* as the basis of a new confession of their own. They made changes to the articles covering the church, the ordinances and the civil magistrate (sometimes following the Savoy Declaration), also slightly altering and extending some other passages. This was published (during a period of fierce persecution) as, *The Second London Confession . . . Put forth by the Elders and Brethren of many congregations of Christians (baptised upon profession of their faith) in London and the country.*

Immediately the period of persecution of Baptists ended this *Confession* was adopted and confirmed by the messengers of Particular Baptist churches who assembled in London in 1689. It became the abiding standard of Particular Baptists.

In the USA the famous *Philadelphia Confession* was derived from the 1689 *Confession*. The Philadelphia Baptist Association officially confirmed its adherence to the 1689 *Confession* in 1724. Then, in 1742, the association added two articles, made some minor alterations and reprinted the *Confession* (Benjamin Franklin was the printer). It became known in the USA as the *Philadelphia Confession*.

The 32 Articles

1. The Holy Scriptures

1. The Holy Scripture is the only sufficient, certain, and infallible rule of all saving knowledge, faith, and obedience.[1] *[How people are saved, the nature of saving faith, and how they must live after they are saved. The word 'sufficient' means that Scripture contains all that we need to know. It deals with every possible issue, and therefore God does not supplement it by inspiring any other agency.]*

Although the light of nature *[natural intelligence]* and the works of creation and providence manifest the goodness, wisdom, and power of God so much that man is left without any excuse *[for his unbelief]*, they are not sufficient to provide that knowledge of God and His will which is necessary for salvation.[2]

Therefore it pleased the Lord at sundry times and in divers manners *[different ways]* to reveal Himself, and to declare His will to His church *[His people]*;[3]

– and afterward, for the better preserving and propagating of the Truth, and for the more sure establishment and comfort of the church, protecting it against the corruption of the flesh *[man's ideas will soon spoil the church]* and the malice of Satan and the world,

– it pleased the Lord to commit His revealed Truth wholly to writing. Therefore the Holy Scriptures are most necessary *[absolutely essential]*, those former ways by which God revealed His will unto His people having now ceased.[4]

1 2 Tim 3.15-17; Isa 8.20; Luke 16.29-31; Eph 2.20.
2 Rom 1.19-21 etc; Rom 2.14-15; Psa 19.1-3.
3 Heb 1.1. **4** Prov 22.19-21; Rom 15.4; 2 Pet 1.19-20.

2. Under the title of Holy Scripture (or the written Word of God) are now contained all the following books of the Old and New Testament:–

OF THE OLD TESTAMENT

Genesis, Exodus, Leviticus, Numbers, Deuteronomy, Joshua, Judges, Ruth, 1 & 2 Samuel, 1 & 2 Kings, 1 & 2 Chronicles, Ezra, Nehemiah, Esther, Job, Psalms, Proverbs, Ecclesiastes, Song of Solomon, Isaiah, Jeremiah, Lamentations, Ezekiel, Daniel, Hosea, Joel, Amos, Obadiah, Jonah, Micah, Nahum, Habakkuk, Zephaniah, Haggai, Zechariah, Malachi.

OF THE NEW TESTAMENT

Matthew, Mark, Luke, John, Acts, Romans, 1 & 2 Corinthians, Galatians, Ephesians, Philippians, Colossians, 1 & 2 Thessalonians, 1 & 2 Timothy, Titus, Philemon, Hebrews, James, 1 & 2 Peter, 1, 2 & 3 John, Jude, Revelation.

All these books are given by the inspiration of God to be the rule of faith and life.[5]

5 2 Tim 3.16.

3. The books commonly called 'The Apocrypha', not being of divine inspiration, are not part of the canon or rule of Scripture and are therefore of no authority to the church of God, nor are they to be approved of *[respected]* or made use of any differently from other human writings.[6]

6 Luke 24.27 & 44; Rom 3.2.

4. The authority of the Holy Scripture, for which it ought to be believed *[which commands our obedience]*, depends not on the testimony of any man or church, but wholly upon God its Author (Who is Truth itself). Therefore it is to be received *[obeyed]* because it is the Word of God.[7]

[In other words, when God speaks, His commands and teachings should not be questioned. We do not believe or obey because a minister proves to us that the teaching is reasonable or rewarding, but because it is God's Word. The Church of Rome claims that the church discerned, gave and guaranteed the Scripture, and that the church alone has the power to interpret. But the Scripture came first, was given by God, is self-authenticating, and rules the church.]

7 2 Pet 1.19-21; 2 Tim 3.16; 1 Thess 2.13; 1 John 5.9.

5. We may be moved and induced by the testimony of the people of God to gain a high and reverent estimation of the Holy Scriptures. We may be similarly affected by the nature of the Scriptures –

– the heavenliness of the contents, the efficacy of the doctrine *[the effectiveness and power of the teaching]*, the majesty of the style, the consent of all the parts *[the perfect agreement of all the parts, devoid of contradiction]*, the scope of the whole, which is to give all glory to God *[unique in literature]*, the full disclosure it makes of the only way of man's salvation, together with many other incomparable excellencies and entire perfections. By all this evidence the Scripture more than proves itself to be the Word of God.

Yet, notwithstanding this, our full persuasion and assurance of the infallible truth of Scripture and its divine authority, is from the inward work of the Holy Spirit bearing witness by and with the Word in our hearts.[8]

8 John 16.13-14; 1 Cor 2.10-12; 1 John 2.20 & 27.

6. The whole counsel *[plan and purpose]* of God concerning all things necessary for His own glory, man's salvation, faith and life, is either expressly set down or necessarily contained in the Holy Scripture, to which nothing is to be added at any time, either by new revelation of the Spirit, or by the traditions of men.[9] *['Necessarily contained' refers to those of God's requirements which are not made in the form of direct commands. Many of these arise as the obvious and logical conclusions which are to be drawn from passages of Scripture.]*

Nevertheless, we acknowledge the inward illumination of the Spirit of God to be necessary for the saving understanding of such things as are revealed in the Word.[10]

There are some circumstances concerning the worship of God and church government which are common to *[all]* human actions *[activities]* and societies, which are to be ordered by the light of nature *[common sense]* and Christian prudence, according to the general rules of the Word which are always to be observed.[11] *[The Scripture does not always give directions for minute and obvious points of conduct or good order.]*

9 2 Tim 3.15-17; Gal 1.8-9. **10** John 6.45; 1 Cor 2.9-12.
11 1 Cor 11.13-14; 1 Cor 14.26 & 40.

7. All things in Scripture are not equally plain in themselves, nor equally clear to everyone,[12] yet those things which are necessary *[essential]* to be known, believed and observed for salvation, are so clearly propounded and revealed in some place of Scripture or other, that not only the educated but also the uneducated may attain a sufficient understanding of them by the due use of ordinary means.[13] *[The means are: listening to the preaching of the Word and reading it with reverence, a teachable spirit, and with prayer. Also, seeking help as necessary from believers.]*

12 2 Pet 3.16. **13** Psa 19.7; Psa 119.130.

8. The Old Testament in Hebrew (which was the native language of

the people of God of old),[14] and the New Testament in Greek (which at the time of its writing was most generally known to the nations) were immediately *[directly]* inspired by God, and were kept pure through subsequent ages by His singular *[extraordinary]* care and providence. They are therefore authentic *[trustworthy]*, so that in all controversies of religion *[doctrinal disputes]*, the church must appeal to them as final.[15]

But because these original tongues are not known to all the people of God who have a right to, and an interest in the Scriptures, and who are commanded to read[16] and search them[17] in the fear of God, the Scriptures are therefore to be translated into the ordinary language of every nation into which they come,[18] so that, with the Word of God living richly in all, people may worship God in an acceptable manner, and through patience and comfort of the Scriptures may have hope.[19]

14 Rom 3.2. **15** Isa 8.20. **16** Acts 15.15. **17** John 5.39.
18 1 Cor 14.6, 9, 11-12, 24, 28. **19** Col 3.16.

9. The infallible rule for the interpretation of Scripture is the Scripture itself, and therefore whenever there is a question about the true and full sense of any scripture (which is not manifold, but one), it must be searched by *[understood in the light of]* other passages which speak more clearly.[20]

[The phrase: 'which is not manifold, but one', means that the Scripture is not merely a library of books, or a collection of important writings or 'insights'. As God's Word, it is one harmonious message without contradiction or confusion. Therefore the practice of interpreting one passage by reference to another is bound to be a trustworthy method of interpretation.]

20 2 Pet 1.20-21; Acts 15.15-16.

10. The supreme judge, by which all controversies of religion are to be determined *[settled]*, and by which must be examined all decrees of councils, opinions of ancient writers, and doctrines of men and private spirits *[individual thinkers]* can be no other than the Holy Scripture, delivered by the Spirit. And in the sentence of Scripture we are to rest *[be satisfied]*, for it is in Scripture, delivered by the Spirit, that our faith is finally resolved.[21] *[The natural man trusts his opinions and his reasoning, but the believer's faith finally trusts the verdict of Scripture.]*

21 Matt 22.29-32; Eph 2.20; Acts 28.23.

2. God and the Holy Trinity

1. The Lord our God is the one and only living and true God;[1] Whose subsistence is in and of Himself[2] *[Whose power to exist is drawn from Himself alone, so that He needs nothing from outside Himself]*;

– Who is infinite *[boundless or endless]* in being and perfection; Whose essence cannot be comprehended *[grasped or understood]* by any but Himself;[3]

– Who is a most pure spirit,[4] invisible, without body, parts, or passions *[emotions which are unstable and which dominate and drive the person – like sexual love, or greed, or human hatred, or temper]*;

– Who only has immortality *[the immortality of others is from Him]*;

– Who dwells in the light which no man can approach,[5] Who is immutable[6] *[unchanging]*, immense[7] *[immeasurable]*, eternal,[8] incomprehensible *[far beyond man's imagination or understanding]*, almighty[9] *[all powerful]*, in every way infinite, most holy,[10] most wise, most free, most absolute *[ie: independent, complete, unmixed with anything]*;

– Who works all things according to the counsel *[plan and purpose]* of His own immutable *[unchanging]* and most righteous will,[11] for His own glory;[12]

– Who is most loving, gracious, merciful, longsuffering, and abundant in goodness and truth;

– Who forgives iniquity *[our condition of moral perversity or crookedness]*, transgression *[rebellion]*, and sin *[actual offences against God's law]*;

– Who is the rewarder of those who diligently seek Him;[13]

– and Who, at the same time, is most just and terrible *[formidable]* in His judgements,[14] hating all sin,[15] and Who will by no means clear the guilty.[16]

1 1 Cor 8.4-6; Deut 6.4. 2 Jer 10.10; Isa 48.12. 3 Exod 3.14. 4 John 4.24.
5 1 Tim 1.17; Deut 4.15-16. 6 Mal 3.6. 7 1 Kings 8.27; Jer 23.23. 8 Psa 90.2.
9 Gen 17.1. 10 Isa 6.3. 11 Psa 115.3; Isa 46.10. 12 Prov 16.4; Rom 11.36.
13 Exod 34.6-7; Heb 11.6. 14 Neh 9.32-33. 15 Psa 5.5-6.
16 Exod 34.7; Nahum 1.2-3.

2. God, having all life,[17] glory,[18] goodness,[19] blessedness, in and from Himself, is unique in being all-sufficient, both in Himself and to Himself, not standing in need of any creature which He has made, nor deriving any glory *[or benefit]* from such.[20]

– On the contrary, it is God Who manifests His own glory in them, through them, to them and upon them. He is the only fountain *[source]* of all being; from Whom, through Whom, and to Whom all things exist and move[21] *[He is the source, the sustainer and the destination of all mankind].*

– He has completely sovereign dominion over all creatures, to do through them, for them, or to them whatever He pleases.[22]

– In His sight all things are open and manifest *[obvious]*;[23] His knowledge is infinite, infallible, and not dependent upon the creature. *[He does not depend upon angels or people for 'reports' of what is happening.]*

– Therefore, nothing is for Him contingent *[dependent upon events]* or uncertain.[24]

– He is most holy in all His counsels *[plans and purposes]*, in all His works,[25] and in all His commands.

– To Him is due from angels and men whatever worship,[26] service, or obedience, they owe as creatures to the Creator, and whatever else He is pleased to require from them.

17 John 5.26. **18** Psa 148.13. **19** Psa 119.68. **20** Job 22.2-3. **21** Rom 11.34-36.
22 Dan 4.25 & 34-35. **23** Heb 4.13. **24** Ezek 11.5; Acts 15.18. **25** Psa 145.17.
26 Rev 5.12-14.

3. In this divine and infinite Being there are three subsistences *[Beings or Persons]*, the Father, the Word or Son, and the Holy Spirit.[27] All are one in substance, power, and eternity *[timelessness]*; each having the whole divine essence, yet this essence being undivided[28] *[all are completely God, yet the Godhead is not divided].*

The Father was not derived from any other being; He was neither brought into being by, nor did He issue from any other being.

– The Son is eternally begotten of the Father.[29]

– The Holy Spirit proceeds from the Father and the Son.[30]

– All three are infinite, without beginning, and are therefore only one God, Who is not to be divided in nature and being *[for there is no difference between the members of the Godhead]*, but distinguished by several peculiar relative properties *[ie: by Their separate and distinctive roles]*, and also Their personal relations *[the mode of family relationships which They adopt].*

– This doctrine of the Trinity is the foundation of all our communion with God, and our comfortable dependence on Him. *[If the members of the Godhead relate to one another in a familiar way, it teaches us that it is God's 'nature' to know and to be known. Thus this doctrine is the foundation of our seeking the Lord for a personal relationship.]*

27 1 John 5.7; Matt 28.19; 2 Cor 13.14. **28** Exod 3.14; John 14.11; 1 Cor 8.6.
29 John 1.14, 18. **30** John 15.26; Gal 4.6.

3. God's Decree
[God's eternal decisions or will; God's directives; God's eternal plan]

1. God has decreed in Himself *[decided by Himself]* from all eternity, by the most wise and holy counsel of His own will, freely and unchangeably, all things which shall ever come to pass.[1] *[Nothing forced Him in the making of any of His plans, and all His intentions will be carried out without the slightest alteration.]*

– Yet in such a way that God is neither the author of sin nor does He have fellowship *[mutual responsibility]* with any[2] in the committing of sins, nor is violence offered to the will of the creature *[no one is made to sin]*, nor yet is the liberty or contingency of second causes taken away, *[ie: nor is the free working of the law of cause and effect interfered with]* but rather established.[3]

– In all this God's wisdom is displayed, disposing all things *[ordering the course of events]*, and also His power and faithfulness in accomplishing His decree.[4] *[God's faithfulness here means – His unswerving conformity to His own holy character and His revealed Word.]*

1 Isa 46.10; Eph 1.11; Heb 6.17; Rom 9.15, 18. **2** James 1.13-15; 1 John 1.5. **3** Acts 4.27-28; John 19.11. **4** Num 23.19; Eph 1.3-5.

2. Although God knows everything which may or can come to pass under all imaginable conditions,[5] yet He has not decreed anything because He foresaw it in the future, or because it would come to pass *[anyway]* under certain conditions.[6]

5 Acts 15.18. **6** Rom 9.11-18.

3. By the decree of God, for the manifestation *[the expression and revealing]* of His glory, some men and angels are predestinated or fore-ordained to eternal life through Jesus Christ,[7] to the praise of His glorious grace.[8] *[ie: so that His glorious grace might be revealed and praised.]* Others are left to act in their sin to their just condemnation, to the praise of His glorious justice.[9] *[ie: so that His glorious justice might be revealed and praised.]*

7 1 Tim 5.21; Matt 25.34. **8** Eph 1.5-6. **9** Rom 9.22-23; Jude 4.

4. Those angels and men thus predestinated and foreordained, are particularly and unchangeably designed *[individually designated]*, and the number of them is so certain and definite, that it cannot be either increased or diminished.[10]

10 2 Tim 2.19; John 13.18.

5. Those of mankind who are predestinated to life, God chose before

the foundation of the world was laid, in accordance with His eternal and immutable *[unchanging]* purpose and the secret counsel and good pleasure of His will. God chose them in Christ for everlasting glory, solely out of His free grace and love,[11] without anything in the creature *[any factor whatsoever]* as a condition or cause moving Him to choose.[12] *[Nothing in the person was taken into consideration.]*

11 Eph 1.4, 9, 11; Rom 8.30; 2 Tim 1.9; 1 Thess 5.9. **12** Rom 9.13-16; Eph 2.5 & 12.

6. As God has appointed the elect unto glory, so, by the eternal and completely free intention of His will, He has foreordained all the means *[of bringing their salvation about]*.[13] Accordingly, those who are elected, being fallen in Adam:

– are redeemed by Christ,[14]

– are effectually called to faith in Christ by His Spirit working in due season,

– are justified, adopted, sanctified,[15]

– and are kept by His power through faith unto salvation;[16]

– neither are any but the elect redeemed by Christ, effectually called, justified, adopted, sanctified, and saved.[17]

13 1 Pet 1.2; 2 Thess 2.13. **14** 1 Thess 5.9-10. **15** Rom 8.30; 2 Thess 2.13.
16 1 Pet 1.5. **17** John 10.26; 17.9; 6.64.

7. The doctrine of this high mystery of predestination is to be handled with special prudence *[discretion]* and care, in order that men who are heeding the will of God revealed in His Word, and who are yielding obedience to it, may, from the certainty of their effectual vocation *[their experience of salvation]* be assured of their eternal election[18] *[their eternal security]*.

So shall this doctrine provide cause for praise,[19] reverence, admiration of God, and also provide cause for humility,[20] diligence, and abundant consolation *[great comfort]* to all who sincerely obey the Gospel.[21]

18 1 Thess 1.4-5; 2 Pet 1.10. **19** Eph 1.6; Rom 11.33.
20 Rom 11.5-6 & 20. **21** Luke 10.20.

4. Creation

1. In the beginning it pleased God the Father, Son, and Holy Spirit,[1] for the manifestation *[expression and revelation]* of the glory of His eternal power,[2] wisdom, and goodness, to create or make the world and all things in it both visible and invisible, in the space of six days, and all very good.[3]

1 John 1.2-3; Heb 1.2; Job 26.13. **2** Rom 1.20. **3** Col 1.16; Gen 1.31.

2. After God had made all other creatures, He created man, male and female,[4] with reasoning and immortal souls,[5] rendering them fit to live that life for Him for which they were created;

– being made in the image of God, in knowledge, righteousness, and true holiness;[6] having the law of God written in their hearts,[7] and having the power to fulfil it;

– and yet living under a possibility of transgressing, being left to the liberty of their own will, which was subject to change[8] *[free to rebel – therefore potentially unstable].*

4 Gen 1.27. **5** Gen 2.7. **6** Ecc 7.29; Gen 1.26. **7** Rom 2.14-15. **8** Gen 3.6.

3. Besides the law written in their hearts, they received a command not to eat of the tree of the knowledge of good and evil.[9] While they kept this command they were happy in their communion with God, and had dominion *[lordship and control]* over all other creatures.[10]

9 Gen 2.17. **10** Gen 1.26, 28.

5. Divine Providence
[God's oversight and benevolent care]

1. God the good Creator of all things, in His infinite power and wisdom, upholds, directs, disposes and governs all creatures and things,[1] from the greatest to the least,[2] by His most wise and holy providence, to the end for which they were created. *[God governs and provides for them in order to fulfil the purpose for which they were created.]*

– God governs *[to fulfil this purpose]* according to His infallible foreknowledge and the free and unchanging counsel of His own will;

– for the praise of the glory of His wisdom, power, justice, boundless goodness, and mercy.[3] *[This last phrase is the 'end' or purpose for which all creatures were created – that God's attributes may be expressed and revealed, and that God may be glorified.]*

1 Heb 1.3; Job 38.11; Isa 46.10-11; Psa 135.6. **2** Matt 10.29-31. **3** Eph 1.11.

2. Although in relation to the foreknowledge and decree *[plan]* of God, Who is the First Cause, all things come to pass immutably and infallibly;[4] so that nothing happens to anyone by chance, or outside His providence,[5] yet by His providence He orders events to occur according to the nature of second causes, either necessarily, freely, or contingently.[6] *[He arranges and permits events to occur through the activity of second causes, such as the laws of nature, or man's free and independent actions, or the activity of market forces, or by the law of 'cause and effect'. God uses and works through such means to bring His purposes to pass.]*

4 Acts 2.23. **5** Prov 16.33. **6** Gen 8.22.

3. God, in His ordinary providence makes use of means[7] *[those just referred to in (2)]*, yet He is free to work outside,[8] above,[9] and against them[10] at His pleasure. *[He can overrule natural laws, human decisions and circumstances when He pleases.]*

7 Acts 27.31 & 44; Isa 55.10-11. **8** Hosea 1.7. **9** Rom 4.19-21. **10** Dan 3.27.

4. The almighty power, unsearchable wisdom, and infinite goodness of God so far manifest themselves *[are so fully expressed]* in His providence, that His determinate counsel *[definite plan]* extends even to the first fall, and all other sinful actions of both angels and men.[11]

– This is not merely by a bare permission, but by a form of permission in which He included the most wise and powerful limitations, and other means of restricting and controlling sin.[12] These various limitations have been designed by God to bring about His most holy purposes.[13]

– Yet, in all these affairs, the sinfulness of both angels and men comes only from them and not from God, Who is altogether holy and righteous, and can never be the author or approver of sin.[14]

11 Rom 11.32-34; 2 Sam 24.1; 1 Chron 21.1. **12** 2 Kings 19.28; Psa 76.10.
13 Gen 50.20; Isa 10.6, 7, 12. **14** Psa 50.21; 1 John 2.16.

5. The most wise, righteous, and gracious God often leaves, for a time, His own children to various temptations, and to the corruptions of their own hearts, in order to chastise them for the sins which they have committed, or to show them the hidden strength of corruption and deceitfulness still in their hearts, so that they may be humbled and aroused to a more close and constant dependence upon Himself for their support, and that they may be made more watchful against future occasions of sin. Other just and holy objectives are also served by such action by God.[15]

Therefore whatever happens to any of His elect is by His appointment, for His glory, and for their good.[16]

15 2 Chron 32.25-31; 2 Cor 12.7-9. **16** Rom 8.28.

6. As for those wicked and ungodly men whom God as a righteous judge, blinds and hardens[17] for former sin, from them He not only withholds His grace, by which they might have been enlightened in their understanding and affected in their hearts,[18] but sometimes He also withdraws the gifts which they had[19] and exposes them to certain objects *[things, or situations]* which their corrupt state will make the occasion of sin.[20] *[They will immediately grasp the opportunity to sin when they are exposed to it.]*

– God gives them over to their own lusts, the temptations of the world, and the power of Satan,[21] so that eventually they harden themselves *[even if placed]* under the same influences which God uses for the softening of others.[22]

17 Rom 1.24-28; 11.7-8. 18 Deut 29.4. 19 Matt 13.12. 20 Deut 2.30; 2 Kings 8.12-13. 21 Psa 81.11-12; 2 Thess 2.10-12. 22 Exod 8.15 & 32; Isa 6.9-10; 1 Pet 2.7-8.

7. As the providence of God in general reaches to all creatures, so, in a more special manner, it takes care of His church *[His people]*, and governs all things to the good of His church.[23]

23 1 Tim 4.10; Amos 9.8-9; Isa 43.3-5.

6. The Fall of Man, Sin and Its Punishment

1. Although God created man upright and perfect, and gave him a righteous law, which secured life for him while he kept it, and although God warned him that he would die if he broke it,[1] yet man did not live long in this honour.
 – Satan using the subtlety of the serpent to subdue Eve, seduced Adam by her, and he, without any compulsion, wilfully transgressed the law of their creation and the command given to them by eating the forbidden fruit.[2]
 – And this act God, according to His wise and holy counsel *[purpose]*, was pleased to permit, having purposed to order it to His own glory.

1 Gen 2.16-17. 2 Gen 3.12-13; 2 Cor 11.3.

2. Our first parents, by this sin, fell from their original righteousness and communion with God, and we in them. *[We fell with them, as a race.]* For from this, death came upon all:[3] all becoming dead in sin[4] and wholly defiled in all the faculties and parts of soul and body.[5]

3 Rom 3.23. 4 Rom 5.12, etc. 5 Tit 1.15; Gen 6.5; Jer 17.9; Rom 3.10-19.

3. They being the root, and by God's appointment, standing in the room and stead *[the place]* of all mankind, the guilt of this sin was imputed *[ascribed]*, and their corrupted nature conveyed, to all their posterity descending from them by ordinary generation[6] *[birth]*. Their descendants are therefore conceived in sin,[7] and are by nature the children of wrath,[8] the servants of sin, and the subjects of death[9] and all other miseries, spiritual, temporal, and eternal, unless the Lord Jesus sets them free.[10]

6 Rom 5.12-19; 1 Cor 15.21-22, 45, 49. 7 Psa 51.5; Job 14.4. 8 Eph 2.3.
9 Rom 6.20 & 5.12. 10 Heb 2.14-15; 1 Thess 1.10.

4. All actual transgressions proceed from this original corruption,[11] by which we are utterly indisposed *[rendered unfit for good]*, disabled, and

made opposite *[averse and antagonistic]* to all good, and wholly inclined to all evil.[12]

11 James 1.14-15; Matt 15.19. **12** Rom 8.7; Col 1.21.

5. During this life the corruption of nature remains in those who are regenerated *[born again]*,[13] and although it is pardoned and mortified *[being put to death]* through Christ, yet this corrupt nature and all its motions *[its initiatives, drives, temptations]* are truly and properly sinful.[14]

13 Rom 7.18, 23; Ecc 7.20; 1 John 1.8. **14** Rom 7.23-25; Gal 5.17.

7. God's Covenant

1. The distance between God and the creature is so great, that although reasonable creatures *[those who have been given the faculty of reason]* do owe obedience to Him as their Creator, yet they could never have attained the reward of life except by some voluntary condescension on God's part, and this He has been pleased to express in the form of a covenant.[1]

1 Luke 17.10; Job 35.7-8.

2. Moreover, as man had brought himself under the curse of the law by his fall, it pleased the Lord to make a covenant of grace.[2] In this covenant He freely offers to sinners life and salvation by Jesus Christ, requiring from them faith in Him that they may be saved,[3] and promising to give to all who are appointed to eternal life His Holy Spirit to make them willing and able to believe.[4]

2 Gen 2.17; Gal 3.10; Rom 3.20-21. **3** Rom 8.3; Mark 16.15-16; John 3.16.
4 Ezek 36.26-27; John 6.44-45; Psa 110.3.

3. This covenant is revealed through the Gospel; first of all to Adam in the promise of salvation by the seed of the woman,[5] and afterwards by further steps until the full revelation of it became complete in the New Testament.[6] This covenant of salvation rests upon an eternal covenant transaction between the Father and the Son about the redemption of the elect.[7] It is solely by the grace *[undeserved mercy and favour]* of this covenant that all the descendants of fallen Adam who have ever been saved have obtained life and blessed *[blissful]* immortality, because man is now utterly incapable of gaining acceptance with God on the terms by which Adam stood in his state of innocency.[8]

5 Gen 3.15. **6** Heb 1.1. **7** 2 Tim 1.9; Tit 1.2.
8 Heb 11.6 & 13; Rom 4.1-2 etc; Acts 4.12; John 8.56.

8. Christ the Mediator

1. It pleased God, in His eternal purpose, to choose and ordain *[appoint]* the Lord Jesus, His only begotten Son, in accordance with the covenant made between them both, to be the Mediator between God and man;[1] to be Prophet[2] *[Teacher]*, Priest[3] *[Mediator]*, and King,[4] the Head and Saviour of His Church,[5] the Heir of all things,[6] and the Judge of all the world.[7] To the Lord Jesus He gave, from all eternity, a people to be His seed *[His children]*. These, in time *[the dispensation of time]*, would be redeemed, called, justified, sanctified, and glorified by the Lord Jesus.[8]

[Redeemed = purchased from bondage by the precious blood of Christ. Called = the personal and irresistible call of the Shepherd. Justified = declared righteous and pardoned in God's sight. Sanctified = healed and changed for holiness by His power. Glorified = finally transformed and invested with perfect beauty when exalted to the glory of Heaven.]

1 Isa 42.1; 1 Pet 1.19-20. **2** Acts 3.22. **3** Heb 5.5-6. **4** Psa 2.6; Luke 1.33.
5 Eph 1.22-23. **6** Heb 1.2. **7** Acts 17.31. **8** Isa 53.10; John 17.6; Rom 8.30.

2. The Son of God, the second person in the Holy Trinity, being true and eternal God, the brightness of the Father's glory, of the same substance *[or essence]* and equal with Him;

– Who made the world, and Who upholds and governs all things which He has made,

– did, when the fulness of time had come *[the time previously fixed by the Godhead]*, take upon Himself man's nature, with all its essential properties and common infirmities,[9] with the exception of sin.[10]

– He was conceived by the Holy Spirit in the womb of the Virgin Mary, the Holy Spirit coming down upon her and the power of the Most High overshadowing her, so that He was born to a woman from the tribe of Judah, a descendant of Abraham and David, in accordance with the Scriptures.[11]

– Thus two whole, perfect and distinct natures were inseparably joined together in one person, without conversion, composition, or confusion;

– So that the Lord Jesus Christ is truly God and truly man, yet He is one Christ, the only Mediator between God and man.[12]

['Without conversion' means that Christ's divine nature was not transformed into humanity, but the latter was added to the divine. Composition means mixing – the two natures could not possibly have been mixed. Confusion did not occur either; in other words there was no disorder, contradiction or incompatibility involved in this sublime joining

of two natures.]

9 John 1.1, 14; Gal 4.4. **10** Rom 8.3; Heb 2.14-17; 4.15.
11 Matt 1.22-23; Luke 1.27, 31, 35. **12** Rom 9.5; 1 Tim 2.5.

3. The Lord Jesus, His human nature thus united to the divine, once in the person of the Son, was sanctified and anointed with the Holy Spirit above measure *[without limit]*,[13] having in Himself all the treasures of wisdom and knowledge.[14] It pleased the Father that all fulness should dwell in Him[15] so that, being holy, harmless, undefiled,[16] and full of grace and truth,[17] He might be thoroughly furnished to execute *[perform]* the office *[function]* of a Mediator and Surety,[18] a position and duty which He did not take upon Himself, but was called to perform by His Father.[19] And the Father also put all power *[as King over the earth]* and judgement *[of mankind]* in His hand, and gave Him commandment to exercise the same.[20]

13 Psa 45.7; Acts 10.38; John 3.34. **14** Col 2.3. **15** Col 1.19. **16** Heb 7.26.
17 John 1.14. **18** Heb 7.22. **19** Heb 5.5. **20** John 5.22 & 27; Matt 28.18; Acts 2.36.

4. This office and duty of Mediator and Surety the Lord Jesus undertook most willingly.[21] To discharge it, He was made under the law *[subject to the law]*,[22] and perfectly fulfilled it, and He underwent the punishment due to us, which we should have borne and suffered.[23] He was made sin and was made a curse for us;[24] enduring the most grievous *[the greatest possible]* sorrows in His soul with the most painful sufferings in His body.[25] He was crucified, and died, and remained in the state of the dead, but His body did not undergo any decomposition.[26] On the third day He rose from the dead with the same[27] body in which He had suffered,[28] with which He also ascended into Heaven,[29] and there sits at the right hand of His Father making intercession *[for His people]*,[30] and shall return to judge men and angels at the end of the world.[31]

21 Psa 40.7-8; Heb 10.5-10; John 10.18. **22** Gal 4.4; Matt 3.15.
23 Gal 3.13; Isa 53.6; 1 Pet 3.18. **24** 2 Cor 5.21.
25 Matt 26.37-38; Luke 22.44; Matt 27.46. **26** Acts 13.37. **27** 1 Cor 15.3-4.
28 John 20.25, 27. **29** Mark 16.19; Acts 1.9-11. **30** Rom 8.34; Heb 9.24.
31 Acts 10.42; Rom 14.9-10; Acts 1.11; 2 Pet 2.4.

5. The Lord Jesus, by His perfect obedience and sacrifice of Himself which He, through the eternal Spirit, once offered up to God *[ie: once for ever]*, has fully satisfied the justice of God,[32] has procured reconciliation, and has purchased an everlasting inheritance in the kingdom of Heaven for all those whom the Father has given to Him.[33]

32 Heb 9.14; 10.14; Rom 3.25-26. **33** John 17.2; Heb 9.15.

6. Although the price of redemption was not actually paid by Christ until after His incarnation, yet the virtue, efficacy *[the certain effect or result]*, and benefit arising from His payment were communicated to the elect in all ages from the beginning of the world through those promises, types, and sacrifices in which He was revealed and signified *[pictured and expressed]* as the seed which should bruise the serpent's head[34] *[the descendant of Adam Who would destroy the devil and sin]*, and also the Lamb slain from the foundation of the world,[35] for He is the same yesterday, and today, and for ever.[36]

34 1 Cor 4.10; Heb 4.2; 1 Pet 1.10-11. **35** Rev 13.8. **36** Heb 13.8.

7. Christ, in His work of Mediator, acts according to both natures, each nature doing that which is proper *[appropriate]* to itself. Yet, because of the unity of His person, that which is proper *[strictly applicable]* to one nature is sometimes in Scripture attributed to the person denominated *[indicated]* by the other nature.[37] *[The proof texts are cases in point. In one, the Son of Man is referred to as coming from Heaven whereas He was not strictly the Son of Man until He was incarnate. In the other, God is referred to as having shed His blood.]*

37 John 3.13; Acts 20.28.

8. To all those for whom Christ has obtained eternal redemption, He certainly and effectually applies and communicates this redemption, making intercession for them,[38] uniting them to Himself by His Spirit, revealing to them in the Word and by the Word the mystery of salvation. He persuades them to believe and obey,[39] governing their hearts by His Word and Spirit,[40] and overcoming all their enemies *[who would take away their eternal life]* by His almighty power and wisdom.[41] This is achieved in such a manner and by such ways as are most consonant to *[perfectly consistent with]* His wonderful and unsearchable dispensation *[His infinitely wise management of the world]*, and it is all by free and absolute *[total]* grace, without any condition foreseen in them *[the elect]* to procure it.[42] *[Christ does not save because He foresaw a worthy deed, or a response of faith coming from the person who would be saved. There is no merit or response at all in any sinner. Christ saves unconditionally.]*

38 John 6.37; 10.15-16; 17.9; Rom 5.10. **39** John 17.6; Eph 1.9; 1 John 5.20.
40 Rom 8.9-14. **41** Psa 110.1; 1 Cor 15.25-26. **42** John 3.8; Eph 1.8.

9. This office of Mediator between God and man is proper only to Christ *[belongs exclusively to Christ]*, Who is the Prophet, Priest, and King of the Church of God, and this office may not be transferred from Him to any other, either in whole or in part.[43] *[Saints, angels, churches or priests cannot share Christ's mediatorial office.]*

43 1 Tim 2.5.

10. This number and order of offices *[Prophet-Priest-King]* is essential. Because of our ignorance we need His prophetic office.[44] Because of our alienation from God and the imperfection of the best of our service, we need His priestly office to reconcile us and present us to God as acceptable.[45] Because of our aversion to, and utter inability to return to God, and for our rescue and keeping from spiritual enemies, we need His kingly office to convince, subdue, draw, uphold, deliver, and preserve us until we reach His heavenly kingdom.[46]

44 John 1.18. **45** Col 1.21; Gal 5.17. **46** John 16.8; Psa 110.3; Luke 1.74-75.

9. Free Will

1. God has indued *[furnished]* the will of man, by nature, with liberty and the power to choose and to act upon his choice. This free will is neither forced, nor destined by any necessity of nature *[any built-in compulsion]* to do good or evil.[1]

1 Matt 17.12; James 1.14; Deut 30.19.

2. Man, in his *[original]* state of innocency, had freedom and power to will and to do that which was good and well-pleasing to God,[2] but he was unstable, so that he might fall from this condition.[3] *[Total freedom inevitably included an element of instability – the freedom to fall if he chose to disobey.]*

2 Ecc 7.29. **3** Gen 3.6.

3. Man, by his fall into a state of sin, has completely lost all ability of will to perform any of the spiritual good which accompanies salvation.[4] As a natural man *[the opposite of a spiritual man]*, he is altogether averse *[opposed]* to spiritual good, and dead in sin.[5] He is not able by his own strength to convert himself, or to prepare himself for conversion[6] *[either to desire or to seek it]*.

4 Rom 5.6; 8.7. **5** Eph 2.1-5. **6** Tit 3.3-5; John 6.44.

4. When God converts a sinner, and translates *[conveys]* him into a state of grace, He frees him from his natural bondage to sin,[7] and by grace alone He enables him freely to will and to do that which is spiritually good.[8] But because of his remaining corruptions he does not only (or perfectly) will that which is good, but also wills that which is evil.[9] *[While the will of a converted person is not yet perfect, it is so restored that it is vastly improved. Before conversion the will has no desire or power to perform spiritual good.]*

7 Col 1.13; John 8.36. **8** Phil 2.13. **9** Rom 7.15-23.

5. The will of man will only be made perfectly and immutably *[unchangeably]* free to will good alone in the state of glory.[10]

10 Eph 4.13.

10. Effectual Calling
[God's effective, irresistible call]

1. Those whom God has predestinated to life, He is pleased in His appointed and accepted time to effectually call[1] by His Word and Spirit, out of that state of sin and death which they are in by nature, to grace and salvation by Jesus Christ.[2] He enlightens their minds spiritually and savingly to understand the things of God.[3] He takes away their heart of stone and gives to them a heart of flesh.[4] He renews their wills, and by His almighty power, causes them to desire and pursue that which is good. He effectually draws them to Jesus Christ,[5] yet in such a way that they come absolutely freely, being made willing by His grace.[6]

1 Rom 8.30; 9.7; Eph 1.10-11; 2 Thess 2.13-14. 2 Eph 2.1-6.
3 Acts 26.18; Eph 1.17-18. 4 Ezek 36.26. 5 Deut 30.6; Ezek 36.27; Eph 1.19.
6 Psa 110.3; Song 1.4.

2. This effectual call is of God's free and special grace alone, not on account of anything at all foreseen in man. It is not made because of any power or agency *[quality or action]* in the creature[7] who is wholly passive in the matter. Man is dead in sins and trespasses until quickened *[made alive]* and renewed by the Holy Spirit.[8] By this he is enabled to answer the call, and to embrace the grace offered and conveyed by it. This enabling power is no less power than that which raised up Christ from the dead.[9]

7 2 Tim 1.9; Eph 2.8. 8 1 Cor 2.14; Eph 2.5; John 5.25. 9 Eph 1.19-20.

3. Infants dying in infancy are regenerated and saved by Christ through the Spirit,[10] Who works when, where, and how He pleases.[11] So also are all elect persons who are incapable of being outwardly called by the ministry of the Word.

10 John 3.3-6. 11 John 3.8.

4. Others are not elected, although they may be called by the ministry of the Word, and may experience some common operations of the Spirit[12] *[a measure of understanding and conviction]*, yet because they are not effectually drawn by the Father, they will not and cannot truly come to Christ and therefore cannot be saved.[13] Much less can men who do not embrace the Christian religion be saved, however diligent they may be to frame their lives according to the light of

nature *[their natural understanding]* and the requirements of the religion they profess.[14]

12 Matt 22.14; 13.20-21; Heb 6.4-5. **13** John 6.44-45 & 65; 1 John 2.24-25.
14 Acts 4.12; John 4.22; 17.3.

11. Justification

1. Those whom God effectually calls He also freely justifies,[1] not by infusing righteousness into them, but by pardoning their sins, and by accounting and accepting them as righteous,[2] not for anything wrought in them, or done by them, but for Christ's sake alone.[3] They are not justified because God reckons as their righteousness either their faith, their believing, or any other act of evangelical obedience. They are justified wholly and solely because God imputes to them *[reckons as their righteousness]* Christ's righteousness. He imputes to them Christ's active obedience to the whole law and His passive obedience in death.[4] They receive Christ's righteousness by faith, and rest *[depend]* on Him. They do not possess or produce this faith themselves, it is the gift of God.[5]

1 Rom 3.24; 8.30. **2** Rom 4.5-8; Eph 1.7. **3** 1 Cor 1.30-31; Rom 5.17-19; Eph 2.8-10.
4 Phil 3.8-9. **5** John 1.12; Rom 5.17.

2. Faith which receives Christ's righteousness and depends on Him is the sole instrument of justification,[6] yet this faith is not alone in the person justified *[it is not the only evidence of salvation]*, but is always accompanied by all the other saving graces *[qualities]*. And it is not a dead faith, but works by love[7] *[and is therefore full of loving gratitude to God, is humbly devoted to Him, and loves to make Him known]*.

6 Rom 3.28. **7** Gal 5.6; James 2.17-26.

3. Christ, by His obedience and death, fully discharged the debt of all those who are justified, and by the sacrifice of Himself through the blood of His cross, underwent instead of them the penalty due to them, so making a proper *[specific]*, real, and full satisfaction to God's justice on their behalf.[8] Yet because He was given by the Father for them, and because His obedience and satisfaction was accepted instead of theirs (and both freely, not because of anything in them)[9], therefore they are justified entirely and solely by free grace, so that both the exact justice and the rich grace of God might be glorified in the justification of sinners.[10]

8 Heb 10.14; 1 Pet 1.18-19; Isa 53.5-6. **9** Rom 8.32; 2 Cor 5.21.
10 Rom 3.26; Eph 1.6-7; 2.7.

4. From all eternity God decreed *[decided, determined]* to justify all the elect,[11] and Christ, in the fulness of time, died for their sins, and rose

again for their justification.[12] Nevertheless, they are not personally justified until the Holy Spirit, in due time, actually applies Christ to them.[13]

11 Gal 3.8; 1 Pet 1.2; 1 Tim 2.6. 12 Rom 4.25. 13 Col 1.21-22; Tit 3.4-7.

5. God continues to forgive the sins of those who are justified,[14] and although they can never fall from the state of justification,[15] yet they may, because of their sins, fall under God's fatherly displeasure.[16] In that condition they will not usually have the light of God's countenance restored to them until they humble themselves, confess their sins, ask for pardon, and renew their *[consistent walk of]* faith and repentance.[17]

14 Matt 6.12; 1 John 1.7-9. 15 John 10.28. 16 Psa 89.31-33.
17 Psa 32.5; Psa 51; Matt 26.75.

6. The justification of believers during the Old Testament period was in all these respects exactly the same as the justification of New Testament believers.[18]

18 Gal 3.9; Rom 4.22-24.

12. Adoption

God has vouchsafed *[guaranteed]*, that in Christ, His only Son, and for His sake, all those who are justified shall be made partakers *[sharers]* of the grace of adoption,[1] by which they are taken into the number of the children of God and enjoy their liberties and privileges.[2] They have His name put upon them,[3] and receive the Spirit of adoption.[4] They have access to the throne of grace with boldness, and are enabled to cry, 'Abba, Father!'[5] They are pitied[6] *[shown caring, compassionate love]*, protected,[7] provided for,[8] and chastened by Him as by a Father,[9] yet they are never cast off,[10] but are sealed to the day of redemption,[11] when they inherit the promises as heirs of everlasting salvation.[12]

1 Eph 1.5; Gal 4.4-5. 2 John 1.12; Rom 8.17. 3 2 Cor 6.18; Rev 3.12. 4 Rom 8.15.
5 Gal 4.6; Eph 2.18. 6 Psa 103.13. 7 Prov 14.26. 8 1 Pet 5.7. 9 Heb 12.6.
10 Isa 54.8-9; Lam 3.31. 11 Eph 4.30. 12 Heb 1.14; 6.12.

13. Sanctification

1. Those who are united to Christ, effectually called, and regenerated, having had a new heart and a new spirit created in them through the virtue *[merit]* of Christ's death and resurrection, are then further sanctified in a very real and personal way.[1] Because of the

virtue of Christ's death and resurrection, and by His Word and Spirit dwelling in them,[2] the dominion of the whole body of sin is destroyed.[3] *[The era of sin's total control over them is ended.]* The different lusts of the body of sin are increasingly weakened and mortified[4] *[put to death – put away]*, and Christ's people are increasingly quickened *[made alive, or lively]* and strengthened in all saving graces *[qualities]*,[5] to practise all true holiness, without which no man shall see the Lord.[6]

1 Acts 20.32; Rom 6.5-6. **2** John 17.17; Eph 3.16-19; 1 Thess 5.21-23. **3** Rom 6.14. **4** Gal 5.24. **5** Col 1.11. **6** 2 Cor 7.1; Heb 12.14.

2. This sanctification extends throughout the whole person,[7] yet it remains imperfect *[or incomplete]* in this life. Some remnants of corruption live on in every part,[8] and from this arises a continuous war between irreconcilable parties – the flesh lusting *[vehement]* against the Spirit, and the Spirit against the flesh.[9]

7 1 Thess 5.23. **8** Rom 7.18 & 23. **9** Gal 5.17; 1 Pet 2.11.

3. In this war, although the remaining corruption for a time may greatly prevail *[predominate]*,[10] yet through the continual supply of strength from the sanctifying Spirit of Christ, the regenerate part overcomes.[11] And so the saints grow in grace, perfecting *[moving towards the accomplishing of]* holiness in the fear of God; pressing after a heavenly life in evangelical obedience to all the commands which Christ as Head and King, in His Word, has prescribed to them.[12]

10 Rom 7.23. **11** Rom 6.14. **12** Eph 4.15-16; 2 Cor 3.18; 7.1.

14. Saving Faith

1. The grace of faith by which the elect are enabled to believe, so that their souls are saved, is the work of the Spirit of Christ in their hearts,[1] and is ordinarily *[normally]* brought into being by the ministry of the Word.[2] It is also increased and strengthened by the work of the Spirit through the ministry of the Word, and also by the administration of baptism and the Lord's Supper, prayer, and other means appointed by God.[3]

1 2 Cor 4.13; Eph 2.8. **2** Rom 10.14-17. **3** Luke 17.5; 1 Pet 2.2; Acts 20.32.

2. By this faith a Christian believes to be true whatever is revealed in the Word because this Word has the authority of God Himself.[4] *[Saving faith causes a person to believe all the Bible to be the Word of God – instinctively and completely.]* Also, by this saving faith, a Christian apprehends *[sees]* an excellency in the Word which is higher than in all

other writings and everything else in the world,[5] because the Word shows forth the glory of God, revealing His attributes, showing the excellency of Christ's nature and offices, and also the power and fulness of the Holy Spirit in His workings and operations.

– So the Christian is enabled to cast his soul upon *[fully trust]* the Truth he has believed,[6] and to see and respond to the different kinds of teaching which different passages of Scripture contain. Saving faith equips him to perceive and obey the commands,[7] hear the threatenings with fear and respect,[8] and to embrace the promises of God for this life and the life to come.[9]

– But the first and most important acts of saving faith are those directly to do with Christ, when the soul accepts, receives, and rests upon Him alone for justification, sanctification and eternal life, by virtue of the covenant of grace.[10]

4 Acts 24.14. **5** Psa 19.7-10; 119.72. **6** 2 Tim 1.12. **7** John 15.14. **8** Isa 66.2.
9 Heb 11.13. **10** John 1.12; Acts 16.31; Gal 2.20; Acts 15.11.

3. This faith, although it differs in degree, and may be weak or strong,[11] even at its very weakest is in an entirely different class and has a different nature (like other aspects of saving grace) from the kind of faith and common grace which is possessed by temporary believers.[12] Therefore, though it may be frequently assailed *[attacked]* and weakened, it gets the victory,[13] growing up in many to the attainment of a full assurance through Christ,[14] Who is both the author and finisher of our faith.[15]

11 Heb 5.13-14; Matt 6.30; Rom 4.19-20. **12** 2 Pet 1.1. **13** Eph 6.16; 1 John 5.4-5.
14 Heb 6.11-12; Col 2.2. **15** Heb 12.2.

15. Repentance and Salvation

1. Those of the elect who are converted in riper years *[adult life]*, having lived some time in the state of nature *[unsaved]*, and in this state served various lusts and pleasures, God gives repentance which leads to life, through an effectual call.[1]

1 Tit 3.2-5.

2. Because there is not one person who does good and commits no sin,[2] and because the best of men may fall into great sins and provocations *[to God]* through the power and deceitfulness of their own indwelling corruption and the prevalency *[superior power]* of temptation, God has mercifully provided in the covenant of grace that when believers sin and fall they shall be renewed *[restored]* through repentance to salvation.[3]

2 Ecc 7.20. **3** Luke 22.31-32.

3. Saving repentance is an evangelical grace[4] by which a person who is made to feel, by the Holy Spirit, the manifold evils of his sin, and being given faith in Christ, humbles himself over his sin with godly sorrow, detestation *[hatred]* of his sin and self-abhorrency *[self-disgust or shame]*.[5] In such repentance the person also prays for pardon and strength of grace, and has a purpose and endeavour *[a striving aim and desire]*, by supplies of the Spirit's power, to walk before God and to totally please Him in all things.[6]

4 Zech 12.10; Acts 11.18. **5** Ezek 36.31; 2 Cor 7.11. **6** Psa 119.6 & 128.

4. As repentance is to be continued through the whole course of our lives, on account of the body of death *[continuing corruption]*, and the motions of it, it is therefore every man's duty to repent of his particular known sins particularly[7] *[ie: of individual sins known to him, naming them and repenting of them]*.

7 Luke 19.8; 1 Tim 1.13-15.

5. Such is the provision which God has made through Christ in the covenant of grace for the preservation of believers in the way of salvation, that although even the smallest sin deserves damnation,[8] yet there is no sin great enough to bring damnation on those who repent.[9] This makes the constant preaching of repentance necessary *[essential]*.

8 Rom 6.23. **9** Isa 1.16-18; 55.7.

16. Good Works

1. Good works are only those works which God has commanded in His holy Word.[1] Works which do not have the warrant *[authorisation]* of Scripture, and are devised by men out of blind zeal, or upon any pretence of *[claim to]* good intentions are not good works.[2] *[Therefore, acts of charity etc, are not, of themselves, good works. Good works begin with obedience to God and the call and commands of Scripture. Unbelievers living in disobedience to them cannot perform good works (see section 7).]*

1 Mic 6.8; Heb 13.21. **2** Matt 15.9; Isa 29.13.

2. Good works, performed in obedience to God's commandments, are these: the fruits and evidences of a true and living faith.[3] By these believers express and show their thankfulness,[4] strengthen their assurance,[5] edify their brethren, adorn the profession of the Gospel *[add beauty of conduct to their verbal testimony]*,[6] stop the mouths of the

adversaries *[silence by their behaviour those who would oppose the Gospel]*, and glorify God,[7] Whose workmanship they are; created in Christ Jesus to perform good works,[8] and to have fruits of holiness which lead to eternal life.[9]

3 James 2.18-22. 4 Psa 116.12-13. 5 1 John 2.3-5; 2 Pet 1.5-11. 6 Matt 5.16.
7 1 Tim 6.1; 1 Peter 2.15; Phil 1.11. 8 Eph 2.10. 9 Rom 6.22.

3. Their ability to do these good works does not in any way come from themselves, but comes wholly from the Spirit of Christ.[10] To enable them to do good works, alongside the graces which they have already received *[at conversion]*, it is necessary for there to be a further real influence of the same Holy Spirit to cause them to will and to do of His good pleasure.[11] But believers are not, on these grounds, to grow negligent, as if they were not bound to perform any duty *[to strive personally]* unless given a special motion *[impulse or motivation]* by the Spirit, but they must be diligent in stirring up the grace of God that is in them.[12]

10 John 15.4-5. 11 2 Cor 3.5; Phil 2.13. 12 Phil 2.12; Heb 6.11-12; Isa 64.7.

4. Those who attain the greatest height which is possible in this life in their obedience to God, are still so far from being able to supererogate *[see below]*, and to do more than God requires, that they fall short of much which they are bound to do in their duty to God.[13]

[Works of supererogation are impossible. These are (according to the Church of Rome) works which achieve a superabundant merit which is more than a person needs and which can go to a 'reserve fund' to be credited to others. The Virgin Mary, according to Rome, accomplished this, and so do many others.]

13 Job 9.2-3; Gal 5.17; Luke 17.10.

5. We cannot by our best works merit *[deserve]* pardon of sin or eternal life from the hand of God because of the great disproportion *[the vast imbalance]* between our best works and the glory to come, and because of the infinite distance which is between us and God. With our works we cannot profit or satisfy God concerning the debt we owe on account of our sins.[14] When we have done all we can *[our very best]*, we have only done our duty, and are still unprofitable servants. And in any case, in so far as our works are good they originate from the work of the Holy Spirit[15] *[and therefore the merit is not truly ours]*. Even then, the good works *[which God Himself has originated]* are so defiled by us, and so mixed with weakness and imperfection, that they could not survive the severity of God's judgement.[16]

14 Rom 3.20; Eph 2.8-9; Rom 4.6. 15 Gal 5.22-23. 16 Isa 64.6; Psa 143.2.

6. Yet, quite apart from the fact that believers are accepted through

Christ as individual souls, their good works are also accepted through Christ.[17] It is not as though the believers are (in this life) wholly unblameable and unreprovable in God's sight, but because He looks upon them in His Son, and is pleased to accept and reward that which is sincere, although it is accompanied with many weaknesses and imperfections.[18]

17 Eph 1.6; 1 Pet 2.5. **18** Matt 25.21-23; Heb 6.10.

7. Works performed by unregenerate men, although they may in essence be things which God commands, and they may be good and beneficial both to themselves and others,[19] yet because they do not proceed from a heart purified by faith,[20] and are not done in a right manner according to the Word,[21] and because it is not their underlying purpose to bring glory to God,[22] therefore they are sinful, and cannot please God, nor can they make a man fit to receive grace from God.[23] And yet, for unregenerate men to neglect such works is even more sinful and displeasing to God.[24]

19 2 Kings 10.30; 1 Kings 21.27-29. **20** Gen 4.5; Heb 11.4-6. **21** 1 Cor 13.1. **22** Matt 6.2-5. **23** Amos 5.21-22; Rom 9.16; Tit 3.5. **24** Job 21.14-15; Matt 25.41-43.

17. The Perseverance of the Saints
[Their persistence or steadfast continuance in the state of grace]

1. Those whom God has accepted in the Beloved *[the Lord Jesus]*, and has effectually called and sanctified by His Spirit, and given the precious faith of His elect, can neither totally *[completely]* nor finally fall from the state of grace, but they will certainly persevere *[definitely persist]* in that state to the end and be eternally saved. This is because the gifts and calling of God are without repentance *[He will never change His mind]*, and therefore He continues to beget *[create]* and nourish in them faith, repentance, love, joy, hope, and all the graces of the Spirit which lead to immortality.[1]

And though many storms and floods arise and beat against the saints, yet these things shall never be able to sweep them off the foundation and rock which they are fastened upon by faith. Even though, through unbelief *[including lack of faith]* and the temptations of Satan, the sight and feeling of the light and love of God may for a time be clouded and obscured from them,[2] yet God is still the same, and they are sure to be kept by His power until their salvation is complete, when they shall enjoy the purchased possession which is theirs, for they are engraved upon the palm of His hands, and their names have been written in His Book of Life from all eternity.[3]

1 John 10.28-29; Phil 1.6; 2 Tim 2.19; 1 John 2.19.
2 Psa 89.31-32; 1 Cor 11.32. **3** Mal 3.6.

2. This perseverance of the saints does not depend on them – that is, on their own free will. It rests upon the immutability *[unchanging character]* of the decree of election,[4] which flows from the free and unchangeable love of God the Father. It also rests upon the efficacy *[the power and certain success]* of the merit and intercession of Jesus Christ *[those for whom He died cannot fail to be saved]*, and upon the union which true saints have with Him[5] *[He will never let His loved ones go]*.

– It rests upon the oath *[solemn affirmation]* of God,[6] and upon the abiding of His Spirit *[Who cannot fail]*.

– It depends upon the seed of God *[which cannot die]* being within them[7] and upon the very nature of the covenant of grace.[8] *[The covenant stipulates that saved souls will never turn away.]*

– All these factors give rise to the certainty and infallibility of the security and perseverance of the saints.

4 Rom 8.30; 9.11-16. **5** Rom 5.9-10; John 14.19. **6** Heb 6.17-18.
7 1 John 3.9. **8** Jer 32.40.

3. The saints may, through the temptation of Satan and the world, and because their remaining sinful tendencies prevail over them, and through their neglect of the means which God has provided to keep them, fall into grievous sins.

They may continue in this state for some time,[9] so that they incur God's displeasure, grieve His Holy Spirit,[10] suffer the impairment of their graces and comforts,[11] have their hearts hardened and their consciences wounded,[12] and hurt and scandalise *[offend]* others. By this they will bring temporal judgements *[present punishment]* upon themselves.[13]

Yet *[despite all this]* they shall *[in time]* renew their repentance and be preserved, through faith in Christ Jesus, to the end.[14]

9 Matt 26.70-74. **10** Isa 64.5-9; Eph 4.30. **11** Psa 51.10-12. **12** Psa 32.3-4.
13 2 Sam 12.14. **14** Luke 22.32 & 61-62.

18. Assurance of Salvation

1. Although temporary believers, and other unregenerate men, may vainly deceive themselves with false hopes and carnal presumptions *[in an unspiritual way they take it for granted]* that they are in the favour of God and in a state of salvation, such a hope on their part will perish *[die away]*.[1] Yet those who truly believe in the Lord Jesus,

and love Him in sincerity, and who endeavour to walk in all good conscience before Him, may be certainly assured in this life that they are in the state of grace, and may rejoice in the hope of the glory of God.[2] And such a hope shall never make them ashamed.[3] *[It will never disappoint them or let them down, for God will bless them, hear their prayers, and finally take them to glory.]*

1 Job 8.13-14; Matt 7.22-23. **2** 1 John 2.3; 3.14-24; 5.13. **3** Rom 5.2-5.

2. This assurance is not merely a conjectural persuasion *[something supposed to be true on slender grounds]* nor even a probable persuasion based upon a fallible hope. It is an infallible assurance of faith[4] founded on the blood and righteousness of Christ revealed in the Gospel.[5] *[It is based on a historical act of the Saviour of the world.]* It is also founded upon the inward evidence of those graces of the Spirit *[marks or evidences of grace]* in connection with definite promises made in the Scriptures,[6] and also on the testimony *[evidence]* of the Spirit of adoption Who witnesses with our spirits that we are the children of God *[a felt, spiritual assurance]*,[7] and Who uses the experience of assurance to keep our hearts both humble and holy.[8]

4 Heb 6.11 & 19. **5** Heb 6.17-18. **6** 2 Pet 1.4-11. **7** Rom 8.15-16. **8** 1 John 3.1-3.

3. This infallible assurance is not so joined to the essence of faith that it is an automatic and inevitable experience. A true believer may wait long and fight with many difficulties before he becomes a partaker of it.[9] Yet, being enabled by the Spirit to know the things which are freely given to him by God, he may, without any extraordinary revelation attain this assurance by using the means of grace in the right way.[10]

Therefore it is the duty of every one to give the utmost diligence to make his calling and election sure, so that his heart may be enlarged in peace and joy in the Holy Spirit, in love and thankfulness to God, and in strength and cheerfulness for carrying out the duties of obedience. These duties are the natural fruits of assurance,[11] for it is far from inclining men to slackness.[12]

9 Isa 50.10; Psa 88; Psa 77.1-12. **10** 1 John 4.13; Heb 6.11-12. **11** Rom 5.1-5; 14.17; Psa 119.32. **12** Rom 6.1-2; Tit 2.11-14.

4. True believers may have the assurance of their salvation in various ways shaken, diminished, or intermitted *[suspended for a time]*. This may be because of their negligence in preserving it,[13] or by their falling into some special sin which wounds the conscience and grieves the Spirit,[14] or by some sudden or forceful temptation,[15] or by God's withdrawing the light of His countenance, and causing even those who fear Him to walk in darkness and to have no light.[16]

Yet, *[whatever the cause or duration of the impairment of assurance]* believers are never left without the seed of God *[essential spiritual identity]*[17] and life of faith *[that hold on eternal values]*,[18] that love of Christ and the brethren, that sincerity of heart and that conscience about their spiritual duty. Out of these things, by the operation of the Spirit, their assurance can in due time be revived,[19] and in the meantime the presence of these graces preserves them from utter despair.[20]

13 Song 5.2-6. **14** Psa 51.8-14. **15** Psa 116.11; 77.7-8; 31.22. **16** Psa 30.7.
17 1 John 3.9. **18** Luke 22.32. **19** Psa 42.5-11. **20** Lam 3.26-31.

19. The Law of God

1. God gave to Adam a law of universal obedience which was written in his heart, and He gave him very specific instruction about not eating the fruit of the tree of knowledge of good and evil.[1] By this Adam and all his descendants were bound to personal, total, exact, and perpetual obedience,[2] being promised life upon the fulfilling of the law, and threatened with death upon the breach of it. At the same time Adam was endued with power and ability to keep it.[3]

1 Gen 2.17; Ecc 7.29. **2** Rom 10.5. **3** Gal 3.10-12.

2. The same law that was first written in the heart of man continued to be a perfect rule of righteousness after the Fall,[4] and was delivered by God upon Mount Sinai in the ten commandments, and written in two tables, the first four containing our duty towards God, and the other six, our duty to man.[5]

4 Rom 2.14-15. **5** Deut 10.4.

3. Besides this law, commonly called the moral law, God was pleased to give the people of Israel ceremonial laws containing several typical ordinances *[rites with symbolical significance, picturing something else]*. These ordinances were partly about their worship, and in them Christ was prefigured *[or represented]* along with His attributes and qualities, His actions, His sufferings and His benefits.[6] These ordinances also gave instructions about different moral duties.[7]

All of these ceremonial laws were appointed only until the time of reformation, when Jesus Christ the true Messiah and the only lawgiver, Who was furnished with power *[authority]* from the Father for this end, cancelled them and took them away.[8]

6 Heb 10.1; Col 2.17. **7** 1 Cor 5.7. **8** Col 2.14-17; Eph 2.14-16.

4. To the people of Israel He also gave sundry judicial laws which expired when they ceased to be a nation. These are not binding on

anyone now by virtue of their being part of the laws of that nation, but their general equity *[their underlying principles of justice and fairness]* continue to be applicable in modern times.[9]

9 1 Cor 9.8-10.

5. The moral law ever binds to obedience everyone, justified people as well as others,[10] and not only out of regard for the matter contained in it, but also out of respect for the authority of God the Creator, Who gave the law.[11] Nor does Christ in the Gospel dissolve this law in any way, but *[on the contrary]* He considerably strengthens our obligation to obey it.[12]

10 Rom 13.8-10; James 2.8-12. **11** James 2.10-11. **12** Matt 5.17-19; Rom 3.31.

6. Although true believers are not under the law as a covenant of works, to be justified or condemned by it,[13] yet it is of great use to them as well as to others, because as a rule of life it informs them of the will of God and their duty and directs and binds them to walk accordingly.

It also reveals and exposes the sinful pollutions of their natures, hearts and lives, and using it for self-examination they may come to greater conviction of sin, greater humility and greater hatred of their sin.[14] They will also gain a clearer sight of their need of Christ and the perfection of His own obedience *[to the law on their behalf]*.

It is of further use to regenerate people *[in self-examination]* to restrain their corruptions *[sinful tendencies]*, because of the way in which it forbids sin. The threatenings of the law serve to show what their sins actually deserve, and what troubles may be expected in this life because of these sins even by regenerate people who are freed from the curse and undiminished rigours of the law.

The promises connected with the law also show believers God's approval of obedience, and what blessings they may expect when the law is kept and obeyed, though blessing will not come to them because they have satisfied the law as a covenant of works. *[To do this would of course require perfect obedience to every part all the time.]* If a man does good and refrains from evil simply because the law encourages to the good and deters him from the evil, that is no evidence that he is under the law rather than under grace.[15]

13 Rom 6.14; Gal 2.16; Rom 8.1; 10.4. **14** Rom 3.20; 7.7, etc.
15 Rom 6.12-14; 1 Pet 3.8-13.

7. The aforementioned uses of the law are not contrary to the grace of the Gospel *[the Gospel of undeserved mercy and favour]*, but they sweetly comply with it,[16] as the Spirit of Christ subdues and enables

the will of man to do freely and cheerfully those things which the will of God, which is revealed in the law, requires to be done.[17]

16 Gal 3.21. **17** Ezek 36.27.

20. The Gospel and Its Influence

1. The covenant of works being broken by sin, and made unprofitable for life *[useless for giving life]*, God was pleased to promise Christ, the seed of the woman *[in Genesis 3]*, as the means of calling the elect and bringing to life within them faith and repentance.[1] In this *[very first]* promise the substance *[all the heart and essential matter]* of the Gospel was revealed and shown to be the effectual *[the valid and effective way]* for the conversion and salvation of sinners.[2]

1 Gen 3.15. **2** Rev 13.8.

2. This promise of Christ and the salvation which comes by Him, is revealed only by the Word of God.[3] The works of creation and providence with the light of nature do not reveal Christ or His grace even in a general or obscure *[shadowy]* way.[4] How much less, therefore, can those who are devoid of the revelation of Christ by the promise (or the Gospel) be enabled by the light of nature *[etc]* to arrive at saving faith or repentance.[5]

3 Rom 1.17. **4** Rom 10.14-17. **5** Prov 29.18; Isa 25.7; 60.2-3.

[The original is here left intact with paraphrase following.]
3. The revelation of the Gospel unto sinners, made in divers times and by sundry parts, with the addition of promises and precepts for the obedience required therein, as to the nations and persons to whom it is granted, is merely of the sovereign will and good pleasure of God,[6] not being annexed by virtue of any promise to the due improvement of men's natural abilities, by virtue of common light received without it, which none ever did make, or can do so;[7] and therefore in all ages, the preaching of the Gospel has been granted unto persons and nations, as to the extent or straitening of it, in great variety, according to the counsel of the will of God.

Paraphrase:–
3. The revelation of the Gospel to sinners, given at different times and in many separate parts, complete with promises and instructions about the response which is required, has been granted to nations and individuals solely according to the sovereign will and good pleasure of God.[6]

It was never granted to them by virtue of their promising (or showing any good intentions) to dedicate their lives to the right things, and change their ways, guided by common sense alone; for no one has ever made such a promise in these circumstances, nor can do so.[7]

Therefore in all ages, the preaching of the Gospel has been granted to individuals and nations, whether to a great extent or a limited extent, (with considerable variation) according to the counsel of the will of God.

6 Psa 147.20; Acts 16.7. **7** Rom 1.18-32.

4. Although the Gospel is the only outward *[external]* means of revealing Christ and saving grace, and as such is totally sufficient to accomplish this, yet more is necessary if men who are dead in trespasses are to be born again, brought to life or regenerated. It is necessary for there to be an effectual, insuperable *[irresistible]* work of the Holy Spirit upon the whole soul *[every part of it]* to produce in them a new spiritual life.[8] Without this no other means will bring about their conversion to God.[9]

8 Psa 110.3; 1 Cor 2.14; Eph 1.19-20. **9** John 6.44; 2 Cor 4.4-6.

21. Christian Liberty and Liberty of Conscience

1. The liberty which Christ has purchased for believers under the Gospel, lies in their freedom from the guilt of sin[1] and the condemning wrath of God, from the rigours and curse of the law, and in their deliverance from this present evil world,[2] from bondage to Satan,[3] from dominion of sin,[4] from the harm of afflictions,[5] from the fear and sting of death, from the victory of the grave,[6] and from everlasting damnation.[7]

– This liberty is also seen in their free access to God, and their ability to yield obedience to Him not out of slavish fear,[8] but with childlike love and willing minds.[9]

All these freedoms were also experienced in substance by true believers under the Old Testament law,[10] but for New Testament Christians this liberty is further enlarged, for they have freedom from the yoke of the ceremonial law to which the Jewish church was subjected. They also have greater boldness of access to the throne of grace and fuller communications of the free Spirit of God than believers under the law normally experienced.[11]

1 Gal 3.13. **2** Gal 1.4. **3** Acts 26.18. **4** Rom 8.3. **5** Rom 8.28.
6 1 Cor 15.54-57. **7** 1 Thess 1.10. **8** Rom 8.15. **9** Luke 1.73-75; 1 John 4.18.
10 Gal 3.9-14. **11** John 7.38-39; Heb 10.19-21.

2. God alone is Lord of the conscience,[12] and has left it free from all doctrines and commandments of men which are in any respect contrary to His Word, or not contained in it.[13] Thus to believe such doctrines or to obey such commands out of conscience, is to betray true liberty of conscience.[14] The requiring of an implicit faith, an absolute and blind obedience, is to destroy liberty of conscience and reason also.[15] *[An 'implicit faith' here refers to a kind of general faith. A person may have faith, for example, in all the teachings of a particular church. He may not exercise an independent faith in any particular doctrine. He accepts a 'package' as part of his faith in the church or system.]*

12 James 4.12; Rom 14.4. **13** Acts 4.19; 5.29; 1 Cor 7.23; Matt 15.9.
14 Col 2.20-23. **15** 1 Cor 3.5; 2 Cor 1.24.

3. They who on pretence of Christian liberty practise any sin, or cherish any sinful lust, pervert the main purpose of the grace of the Gospel to their own destruction.[16] They completely destroy the object of Christian liberty, which is that we, being delivered out of the hands of all our *[spiritual]* enemies, might serve the Lord without fear, in holiness and righteousness before Him, all the days of our lives.[17] *[Some have claimed the doctrine of Christian liberty as a protection against being challenged over sin or disorderly conduct. The object of liberty is to bring us to serve and obey God more, but without spiritual bondage.]*

16 Rom 6.1-2. **17** Gal 5.13; 2 Pet 2.18-21.

22. Worship and the Sabbath Day

1. The light of nature shows that there is a God Who has lordship and sovereignty over all, is just and good, and Who does good to all. Therefore He is to be feared, loved, praised, called upon, trusted in, and served, with all the heart and all the soul, and with all the might.[1] But the acceptable way of worshipping the true God has been instituted by Himself,[2] and therefore our method of worship is limited by His own revealed will. He may not be worshipped according to the imagination and devices of men, nor the suggestions of Satan. He may not be worshipped by way of visible representations *[idols, statues, pictures, etc]*, or by any other way not prescribed in the Holy Scriptures.[3]

1 Jer 10.7; Mark 12.33. **2** Deut 12.32. **3** Exod 20.4-6.

2. Worship is to be given to God the Father, Son, and Holy Spirit, and to Him alone;[4] not to angels, saints, or any other creatures.[5] And since the Fall, worship is not to be given without a mediator,[6] nor by any

other mediation than that of Christ.[7]

4 Matt 4.9-10; John 4.23; Matt 28.19. **5** Rom 1.25; Col 2.18; Rev 19.10.
6 John 14.6. **7** 1 Tim 2.5.

3. Prayer, with thanksgiving, is one part of natural worship, and this God requires of all men.[8] But to be accepted it must be made in the name of the Son,[9] by the help of the Spirit,[10] and according to His will.[11] It must be made with understanding, reverence, humility, fervency, faith, love, and perseverance; and corporate prayer must be made in a known language.[12] *[In this point the Confession has in mind the Latin liturgy, but the principle applies equally to the charismatic use of tongues in corporate prayer.]*

8 Psa 95.1-7; 65.2. **9** John 14.13-14. **10** Rom 8.26. **11** 1 John 5.14. **12** 1 Cor 14.16-17.

4. Prayer is to be made for lawful things, and for all kinds of people who are alive now or who shall live in the future,[13] but not for the dead,[14] nor for those who are known to have sinned the 'sin leading to death'.[15]

13 1 Tim 2.1-2; 2 Sam 7.29. **14** 2 Sam 12.21-23. **15** 1 John 5.16.

5. The reading of the Scriptures,[16] preaching and hearing the Word of God,[17] the teaching and admonishing of one another in psalms, hymns, and spiritual songs, singing with grace in our hearts to the Lord;[18] as well as the administration of baptism[19] and the Lord's Supper,[20] are all parts of the worship of God. These are to be performed in obedience to Him, with understanding, faith, reverence and godly fear. Also to be used in a holy and reverent manner on special occasions are times of solemn humiliation, fastings,[21] and thanksgivings.[22]

16 1 Tim 4.13. **17** 2 Tim 4.2; Luke 8.18. **18** Col 3.16; Eph 5.19. **19** Matt 28.19-20.
20 1 Cor 11.26. **21** Esther 4.16; Joel 2.12. **22** Exod 15.1-19; Psa 107.

6. Under the Gospel *[the New Testament order]* neither prayer nor any other part of religious worship is tied to, or made more acceptable by, any place in which it is performed or towards which it is directed. God is to be worshipped everywhere in spirit and in truth,[23] whether in private families[24] daily,[25] in secret by each individual,[26] or solemnly in the public assemblies. These are not to be carelessly or wilfully neglected or forsaken, when God by His Word and providence calls us to them.[27]

23 John 4.21; Mal 1.11; 1 Tim 2.8. **24** Acts 10.2. **25** Matt 6.11; Psa 55.17.
26 Matt 6.6. **27** Heb 10.25; Acts 2.42.

7. As it is the law of nature that in general a proportion of time, by God's appointment, should be set apart for the worship of God, so

He has given in His Word a positive, moral and perpetual commandment, binding upon all men, in all ages to this effect. He has particularly appointed one day in seven for a sabbath to be kept holy for Him.[28] From the beginning of the world to the resurrection of Christ this was the last day of the week, and from the resurrection of Christ it was changed to the first day of the week and called the Lord's Day.[29] This is to be continued until the end of the world as the Christian Sabbath, the observation of the last day of the week having been abolished.

28 Exod 20.8. **29** 1 Cor 16.1-2; Acts 20.7; Rev 1.10.

8. The Sabbath is kept holy to the Lord by those who, after the necessary preparation of their hearts and prior arranging of their common *[ordinary or domestic]* affairs, observe all day a holy rest from their own works, words and thoughts about their worldly employment and recreations,[30] and give themselves over to the public and private acts of worship for the whole time, and to carrying out duties of necessity and mercy.[31]

30 Isa 58.13; Neh 13.15-22. **31** Matt 12.1-13.

23. Lawful Oaths and Vows

[Note: an oath is a solemn affirmation of something, or a promise to perform, which is made to (or between) people, while God is invoked as a witness. A vow is a solemn and binding promise made to God.]

1. A lawful oath is an act of religious worship, in which the person swearing in truth, righteousness, and *[sincere]* judgement, solemnly calls God to witness what he swears,[1] and to judge him according to the truth or falsity of it.[2]

1 Exod 20.7; Deut 10.20; Jer 4.2. **2** 2 Chron 6.22-23.

2. Only by the name of God can a righteous oath be sworn, and only if it is used with the utmost fear of God and reverence. Therefore, to swear vainly or rashly by the glorious and awesome name of God, or to swear by any other name or thing, is sinful, and to be regarded with disgust and detestation.[3] But in matters of weight and moment, for the confirmation *[reinforcement]* of truth, and for the ending of strife, an oath is sanctioned by the Word of God.[4] Therefore a lawful oath being imposed by a lawful authority, can rightly be taken in such circumstances.[5]

[In the ending of strife in a church the parties may be required by the elders to solemnly pledge themselves before God to honour a righteous path

in the future. A talebearer may in serious circumstances be required to affirm the truthfulness of his testimony before God. An oath has been further defined as – 'Calling upon God to witness the truth of what we affirm as true; or our voluntary assumption of an obligation to do something in the future – with an implied imprecation of God's disfavour if we lie or prove unfaithful to our engagements.']

3 Matt 5.34-37; James 5.12. **4** Heb 6.16; 2 Cor 1.23. **5** Neh 13.25.

3. Whoever takes an oath sanctioned by the Word of God is bound to consider the weightiness of so solemn an act, and affirm or confess to nothing except that which he knows to be true. For by rash, false, and vain oaths, the Lord is provoked, and because of them this land mourns.[6] *[Empty and insincere oaths and pledges by monarchs and so-called religious leaders and clergy line the road of spiritual compromise, apostasy and decline in our land.]*

6 Lev 19.12; Jer 23.10.

4. An oath is to be taken in the plain and common sense of the words, without equivocation *[ambiguity or double sense]* or mental reservation.[7]

7 Psa 24.4.

5. A vow, which is not to be made to any creature, but to God alone, is to be made and performed with all the utmost care and faithfulness.[8] But monastical vows (as in the Church of Rome) of a perpetual single life,[9] professed poverty,[10] and regular obedience, so far from being degrees of higher perfection, are superstitious and sinful snares, in which no Christian may entangle himself.[11]

8 Psa 76.11; Gen 28.20-22. **9** 1 Cor 7.2 & 9. **10** Eph 4.28. **11** Matt 19.11.

24. The Civil Magistrate

1. God, the supreme Lord and King of all the world, has ordained civil magistrates *[authorities]* to be under Him, over the people, for His own glory and the public good. For this purpose He has armed them with the power of the sword *[the authority to use force]*, for the defence and encouragement of those that do good *[for the safety of, and as an incentive to, law-abiding citizens]*, and for the punishment of evil-doers.[1]

1 Rom 13.1-4.

2. It is lawful for Christians to accept and carry out the duties of a magistrate *[a term covering all public office]* when called upon. In the

performance of such office they are particularly responsible for maintaining justice and peace[2] by application of the right and beneficial laws of the nation. Also, to maintain justice and peace, they may lawfully (under the New Testament) engage in war if it is just and essential.[3]

2 2 Sam 23.3; Psa 82.3-4. **3** Luke 3.14.

3. Because civil magistrates [authorities] are established by God for the purposes previously defined, we ought to be subject to all their lawful commands [legislation] as part of our obedience to God, not only to avoid punishment, but for conscience sake.[4] We ought also to make supplications and prayers for rulers and all that are in authority, that under them we may live a quiet and peaceable life, in all godliness and honesty.[5]

4 Rom 13.5-7; 1 Pet 2.17. **5** 1 Tim 2.1-2.

25. Marriage

1. Marriage is to be between one man and one woman. It is not lawful for any man to have more than one wife, nor for any woman to have more than one husband, at the same time.[1]

1 Gen 2.24; Mal 2.15; Matt 19.5-6.

2. Marriage was ordained for the mutual help of husband and wife,[2] for the increase of mankind with a legitimate issue,[3] *[children are to be born into families as organised by the plan of God]* and for preventing uncleanness[4] *[immorality]*.

2 Gen 2.18. **3** Gen 1.28. **4** 1 Cor 7.2 & 9.

3. It is lawful for all sorts of people to marry if they are able with judgement *[if they are rational]* to give their consent.[5] But it is the duty of Christians to marry in the Lord,[6] and therefore those who profess the true religion should not marry with infidels or idolaters. Nor should those who are godly be unequally yoked by marrying with those who are wicked in their life or who maintain heretical teaching condemned to judgement *[by God's Word]*.[7]

5 Heb 13.4; 1 Tim 4.3. **6** 1 Cor 7.39. **7** Neh 13.25-27.

4. Marriage ought not to be within the degrees of consanguinity or affinity *[blood relationships and close relationships]* forbidden in the Word,[8] nor can such incestuous marriages ever be made lawful by any law of man or consent of parties so that such persons may live together as man and wife.[9]

8 Lev 18. **9** Mark 6.18; 1 Cor 5.1.

26. The Church

1. The universal Church, which may be called invisible (in respect of the internal work of the Spirit and truth of grace) consists of the entire number of the elect, all those who have been, who are, or who shall be gathered into one under Christ, Who is the Head. This universal Church is the wife, the body, the fulness of Him Who fills all in all.[1]

[ie: the universal Church is the true Church of the elect and must be regarded as invisible, because the purest Gospel churches may have in their memberships professing Christians who are hypocritical, mistaken or deluded with regard to their spiritual standing. Equally, the Lord has true believers isolated in unlikely environments. The 'truth of grace' refers to the reality of conversion.]

1 Heb 12.23; Col 1.18; Eph 1.10 & 22-23; 5.23-32.

2. All people throughout the world who profess the faith of the Gospel and obedience to Christ on its terms, and who do not destroy their profession by any errors which contradict or overthrow Gospel fundamentals, or by unholy behaviour, are visible saints and may be regarded as such.[2] All individual congregations ought to be constituted of such people[3] *[as far as we can ensure].*

2 1 Cor 1.2; Acts 11.26. **3** Rom 1.7; Eph 1.20-22.

3. The purest churches under Heaven are subject to *[liable to be affected by]* mixture and error,[4] and some have degenerated so much that they have ceased to be churches of Christ and have become synagogues of Satan.[5] Nevertheless Christ always has had, and always will (to the end of time) have a kingdom in this world, made up of those who believe in Him, and make profession of His name *[witness for Him].*[6]

4 1 Cor 5; Rev 2 & 3. **5** Rev 18.2; 2 Thess 2.11-12.
6 Matt 16.18; Psa 72.17; Psa 102.28; Rev 12.17.

4. The Lord Jesus Christ is the Head of the Church. In Him, by the appointment of the Father, is vested in a supreme and sovereign manner all power *[authority]* for the calling *[forming]*, institution, order, or government of the Church.[7]

The Pope of Rome cannot in any sense be head of the Church, but he is that antichrist, that man of sin, and son of perdition, who exalts himself in the church against Christ and all that is called God, who the Lord shall destroy with the brightness of His coming.[8]

7 Col 1.18; Matt 28.18-20; Eph 4.11-12. **8** 2 Thess 2.3-9.

[This last paragraph is regarded by many who affirm this Confession, as the only debatable statement. There is no disagreement among them as to the heresy and darkness of the Church of Rome, nor of its instrumentality as a tool of Satan down the ages. The papal system is certainly utterly anti-Christian in spirit, form and effect. The issue is – will the last pope of time be a servant of the coming antichrist or will he be antichrist himself? Or, will the Church of Rome prove to be the antichrist? The 'man of sin' may turn out to be a person or even an atheistic ideology, but very few teachers today are prepared to make a definite identification. However, at the very least it must be said that the office of the 'Pope of Rome' is in the power of antichrist, and any serving pope is a man of sin and a son of perdition who exalts himself against the true Word and the message of grace.]

5. In the exercise of the authority which has been entrusted to Him, the Lord Jesus calls to Himself from out of the world, through the ministry of His Word, by His Spirit, those who are given to Him by His Father,[9] so that they may walk before Him in all the ways of obedience which He prescribes to them in His Word.[10] Those who are thus called, He commands to walk together in particular *[individual]* societies or churches, for their mutual edification *[spiritual benefit]*, and for the due performance of that public worship, which He requires of them in the world[11] *[ie: while in the world].*

9 John 10.16; John 12.32. **10** Matt 28.20. **11** Matt 18.15-20.

6. The members of these churches are saints because they have been *[personally and individually]* called by Christ, and because they visibly *[obviously]* manifest and give evidence of their obedience to that call by their profession and walk.[12] Such saints willingly consent to walk together according to the appointment *[instructions]* of Christ, giving themselves up to the Lord and to one another, according to God's will, in avowed subjection to the ordinances *[commands]* of the Gospel.[13] *[True saints are not reserved and remote members of churches. The Lord and His cause is genuinely first in their lives for they have given themselves up to Him and to their fellow believers.]*

12 Rom 1.7; 1 Cor 1.2. **13** Acts 2.41-42; 5.13-14; 2 Cor 9.13.

7. To each of these churches thus gathered, according to the Lord's mind as declared in His Word, He has given all the power and authority which is in any way required for them to carry on the order *[or pattern]* of worship and discipline which He has instituted *[organised and laid down]* for them to observe. He has also given all the commands and rules for the due and right exercise of this power.[14]

14 Matt 18.17-18; 1 Cor 5.4-5; 5.13; 2 Cor 2.6-8.

[Because all the power and authority 'which is in any way required' is

given to local churches, there is no function left for synods, councils, annual assemblies, area superintendents, episcopal bishops, general secretaries, or any other kind of denominational authority. The Lord directly and person-ally governs and empowers local churches, which are humanly autonomous, independent and self-governing. This article also affirms that the New Testa-ment provides a clear pattern for all the legitimate activities and the government of the Lord's churches, a fact disregarded by so many.]

8. A particular church *[an individual congregation belonging to Christ]* gathered and completely *[properly]* organised according to the mind of Christ, consists of officers and members. The officers appointed by Christ to be chosen and set apart by the church are bishops or elders *[the same office]* and deacons. These are to be appointed for the pecu-liar *[exclusive or special]* administration of ordinances *[baptism and the Lord's Supper]* and the execution *[carrying out]* of power or duty *[leader-ship work and special ministries such as teaching and discipline]* with which the Lord has entrusted them and to which He has called them. This pattern of church order is to be continued to the end of the world.[15]

15 Acts 20.17 & 28; Phil 1.1

[The Confession holds strongly to the principle of a responsible leadership in the local church. Such a leadership must be trusted to function, and be obeyed for the sake of its work, as the New Testament eldership texts show, but it may not 'lord it' over God's heritage. Their work includes the task of bringing the entire fellowship to stand committed to the ministries of the church. The key point is that the Confession does not affirm the extreme 'con-gregational' view of church government espoused by later Arminian and 'General' Baptists. The biblical balance and distribution of 'decision' between the church meeting and the officers' courts was clearly seen and practised in the days of this Confession.]

9. The way appointed by Christ for the calling of any person fitted *[qualified]* and gifted by the Holy Spirit for the office of bishop or elder in a church, is that he is to be chosen by the common consent and vote of the church itself.[16] Such a person should be solemnly set apart by fasting and prayer, with the laying on of hands of the eldership of the church (if there be any previously appointed elder or elders).[17] The way of Christ for the calling of a deacon is that he is also to be chosen by the common consent and vote of the church and set apart by prayer, with the laying on of hands.[18]

16 Acts 14.23. **17** 1 Tim 4.14. **18** Acts 6.3-6.

10. Because the work of pastors is to apply themselves constantly to the service of Christ in His churches by the ministry of the Word and

prayer, and by watching for their souls as they that must give an account to Him,[19] the churches to which they minister have a pressing obligation to give them not only all due respect, but also to impart to them a share of all their good things *[material provisions]*, according to their ability.[20]

This must be so done that the pastors may have a comfortable supply *[be so provided for that they are delivered from hardship, pain and trouble]* and that they may not have to be entangled in secular affairs,[21] and may also be able to exercise hospitality towards others.[22] All this is required by the law of nature and by the express command of our Lord Jesus, Who has ordained that they that preach the Gospel should live by the Gospel.[23]

19 Acts 6.4; Heb 13.17. **20** 1 Tim 5.17-18; Gal 6.6-7. **21** 2 Tim 2.4. **22** 1 Tim 3.2. **23** 1 Cor 9.6-14.

11. Although an obligation lies on the elders or pastors of the churches to be urgently preaching the Word by virtue of their office, yet the work of preaching the Word is not exclusively confined to them. Therefore others who are also gifted and qualified by the Holy Spirit for the task, and who are approved and called by the church, may and ought to perform it.[24]

24 Acts 11.19-21; 1 Pet 4.10-11.

12. All believers are bound *[obligated]* to join themselves to particular churches when and where they have opportunity so to do, and all who are admitted into the privileges of a church, are also under the censures *[reproofs]* and government of that church, in accordance with the rule of Christ.[25]

25 1 Thess 5.14; 2 Thess 3.6 & 14-15.

13. No church members, because of any offence which has been given them by a fellow member, once they have performed their prescribed duty towards the person who has caused the offence, may disturb church order in any way, or be absent from the meetings of the church or the administration of any ordinances *[baptism and the Lord's Supper]* on account of any such offence *[sense of grievance]*. On the contrary, they are to wait upon Christ in the further proceedings of the church.[26] *[They must report the matter to Christ's appointed officers for the implementation of church discipline.]*

26 Matt 18.15-17; Eph 4.2-3.

14. Each church and all its members are obligated to pray constantly for the good and prosperity of all Christ's churches everywhere,[27] and to help forward everyone *[like the travelling believers referred to in the proof texts]* who comes into their district or calling, *[probably a*

reference to their trade or business circles] by the exercise of their gifts and graces *[spiritual qualities].*

It clearly follows that when churches are planted by the goodness of God they ought also to hold fellowship among themselves to promote peace, increasing love and mutual edification *[spiritual benefit]* as and when they enjoy an opportunity to do so to their advantage.[28]

27 Eph 6.18; Psa 122.6. **28** Rom 16.1-2; 3 John 8-10.

15. In cases of difficulties or differences, either in matters of doctrine or administration *[church government or methods]*, which concern the churches in general or any single church, and which affects their peace, union, and edification, or when any members of a church are injured because of any disciplinary proceedings not consistent with the Word and correct order, it is according to the mind of Christ, that many churches holding communion together *[sharing the same doctrine]* do, through their appointed messengers *[representatives]* meet to consider, and give their advice about the matter in dispute, and to report to all the churches concerned.[29]

However, when these messengers are assembled, they are not entrusted with any real church power, or with any jurisdiction over the churches involved in the problem. They cannot exercise any censure over any churches or persons, or impose their determination *[conclusions or solutions]* on the churches or their officers.[30]

29 Acts 15.2-6, 22-25. **30** 2 Cor 1.24; 1 John 4.1.

27. The Communion of Saints
[The fellowship and sharing together of the saints]

1. All saints who are united to Jesus Christ, their Head, by His Spirit, and by faith, although they are not by this made one person with Him, have fellowship in His graces, sufferings, death, resurrection, and glory.[1] *[They receive and enjoy real and eternal benefits from all these.]*

Also, being united to one another in love, they have communion *[they share]* in each other's gifts and graces,[2] and are obligated to the orderly performance of such public and private duties *[the services listed in the proof texts]* as lead to their mutual good, both in the inward and outward man *[spiritually and physically].*[3]

['Orderly' here has in mind the 'unruly' people of 1 Thess 5.14. All is to be done in the context of a properly regulated fellowship.]

1 1 John 1.3; John 1.16; Phil 3.10; Rom 6.5-6. **2** Eph 4.15-16; 1 Cor 12.7; 3.21-23.
3 1 Thess 5.11, 14; Rom 1.12; 1 John 3.17-18; Gal 6.10.

2. Saints, by their profession *[that they belong to Christ and His kingdom]* are bound *[committed]* to maintain a holy fellowship and communion in the worship of God and in performing such other spiritual services as advance their mutual edification *[spiritual benefit]*.[4] They are also to give relief to each other in outward things *[alleviate pain, distress or anxiety]* according to their different needs and abilities to meet them.[5]

This communion or fellowship, though chiefly exercised by saints in their immediate circle of fellow believers such as families,[6] and churches,[7] is also to be extended (according to the rule of the Gospel) to all the household of faith, as God gives the opportunity. This means all those who in every place call upon the name of the Lord Jesus. However, their communion with one another as saints does not take away or infringe the personal ownership which each man has of his goods and possessions.[8]

4 Heb 10.24-25; 3.12-13. **5** Acts 11.29-30. **6** Eph 6.4. **7** 1 Cor 12.14-27.
8 Acts 5.4; Eph 4.28.

28. Baptism and the Lord's Supper

1. Baptism and the Lord's Supper are ordinances of positive and sovereign institution, appointed by the Lord Jesus, the only lawgiver, to be continued in His Church to the end of the world.[1] *['Positive' here means that these ordinances are not merely implied in Scripture, but definitely, positively commanded. They are explicitly laid down by Christ.]*

1 Matt 28.19-20; 1 Cor 11.26.

2. These holy appointments are to be administered only by those who are qualified and called to administer them, according to the commission of Christ.[2]

2 Matt 28.19; 1 Cor 4.1.

29. Baptism

1. Baptism is an ordinance of the New Testament, ordained by Jesus Christ, to be to the person who is baptised – a sign of his fellowship with Christ in His death and resurrection; of his being engrafted into Christ;[1] of remission *[forgiveness]* of sins;[2] and of that person's giving up of himself to God, through Jesus Christ, to live and walk in newness of life.[3]

1 Rom 6.3-5; Col 2.12; Gal 3.27. **2** Mark 1.4; Acts 22.16. **3** Rom 6.4.

2. Those who actually profess repentance towards God, faith in, and obedience to, our Lord Jesus Christ, are the only proper *[rightful or correct]* subjects for this ordinance.[4]

4 Mark 16.16; Acts 8.36-37; 2.41; 8.12; 18.8.

3. The outward element to be used in this ordinance is water, in which the person is to be baptised in the name of the Father, and of the Son, and of the Holy Spirit.[5]

5 Matt 28.19-20; Acts 8.38.

4. Immersion – the dipping of the person in water – is necessary *[essential]* for the due *[rightful or adequate]* administration of this ordinance.[6]

6 Matt 3.16; John 3.23.

30. The Lord's Supper

1. The Supper of the Lord Jesus was instituted by Him the same night on which He was betrayed to be observed in His churches until the end of the world for the perpetual remembrance, and showing forth of the sacrifice of Himself in His death.[1]

It was also instituted by Christ to confirm believers in all the benefits of His death;

– for their spiritual nourishment and growth in Him;

– for their further engagement in and commitment to all the duties which they owe to Him;

– and to be a bond and pledge of their communion with Him and with their fellow believers.[2]

1 1 Cor 11.23-26. **2** 1 Cor 10.16-21.

2. In this ordinance Christ is not offered up to His Father, nor is there any real sacrifice made at all for remission of sin (of the living or the dead). There is only a memorial of that one offering up of Christ by Himself upon the cross once for all,[3] the memorial being accompanied by a spiritual oblation *[offering]* of all possible praise to God for Calvary.[4]

Therefore, the popish *[Roman Catholic]* sacrifice of the mass, as they call it, is most abominable *[both spiritually and physically loathsome]*, being injurious to Christ's own sacrifice, which is the only propitiation *[appeasement; atonement]* for all the sins of the elect.

3 Heb 9.25-28. **4** 1 Cor 11.24; Matt 26.26-27.

3. The Lord Jesus has, in this ordinance, appointed His ministers to

pray and bless the elements of bread and wine (so setting them apart from a common to a holy use) and to take and break the bread, then to take the cup, and to give both to the communicants, also communicating themselves[5] *[at the same time]*.

5 1 Cor 11.23-26, etc.

4. The denial of the cup to the people, the practices of worshipping the elements, lifting them up or carrying them about for adoration, or reserving them for any pretended religious use, are all contrary to the nature *[and meaning]* of this ordinance, and to the institution of Christ.[6]

6 Matt 26.26-28; 15.9; Exod 20.4-5.

5. The outward elements in this ordinance which are correctly set apart and used as Christ ordained, so closely portray Him as crucified, that they are sometimes truly (but figuratively) referred to in terms of the things they represent, such as the body and blood of Christ.[7] However *[while such terms may rightly be used of the elements]* in substance and nature they still remain truly and only bread and wine as they were before.[8]

7 1 Cor 11.27. **8** 1 Cor 11.26-28.

6. The doctrine commonly called transubstantiation, which maintains that a change occurs in the substance of the bread and wine into the substance of Christ's body and blood, when consecrated by a priest or by any other way, is repugnant not only to Scripture[9] but even to common sense and reason. It overthrows the nature of the ordinance, and both has been and is the cause of a host of superstitions and of gross idolatries[10] *[repulsively glaring worship of an image of Deity, which is prohibited and condemned by the Lord.]*

9 Acts 3.21; Luke 24.6 & 39. **10** 1 Cor 11.24-25.

7. Worthy receivers, outwardly taking the visible elements in this ordinance, also receive them inwardly and spiritually by faith, truly and in fact, but not carnally and corporally *[they do not receive real human flesh]*, and feed upon Christ crucified, and all the benefits of His death. The body and blood of Christ is not present corporally *[as material body]* or carnally *[as physical flesh]* but it is spiritually present to the faith of believers in the ordinance, just as the elements are present to their outward senses.[11]

11 1 Cor 10.16; 11.23-26.

8. All ignorant and ungodly persons who are unfit to enjoy communion with Christ are equally unworthy of the Lord's Table, and therefore cannot, without great sin against Him, take a share in these

holy mysteries or be admitted to the Supper, while they remain in that condition.[12] Indeed, those who receive (the elements) unworthily, are guilty of the body and blood of the Lord, eating and drinking judgement to themselves.[13]

12 2 Cor 6.14-15. **13** 1 Cor 11.29; Matt 7.6.

31. Man's State After Death, and the Resurrection

1. The bodies of men after death return to dust, and undergo corruption[1] *[decomposition]*, but their souls, which neither die nor sleep *[they do not become unconscious]*, having an immortal subsistence *[means of existence]*, immediately return to God Who gave them.[2]

The souls of the righteous are then made perfect in holiness, are received into paradise where they are with Christ, and look upon the face of God in light and glory, waiting for the full redemption of their bodies.[3]

The souls of the wicked are cast into hell, where they remain in torment and under darkness, reserved to the judgement of the great day.[4] The Scripture acknowledges no other place *[or state]* than these two for souls separated from their bodies.

1 Gen 3.19; Acts 13.36. **2** Ecc 12.7. **3** Luke 23.43; 2 Cor 5.1 & 6-8; Phil 1.23; Heb 12.23. **4** Jude 6-7; 1 Pet 3.19; Luke 16.23-24.

2. At the last day, those of the saints who are still alive shall not sleep *[will not die]* but shall be changed.[5] And all the dead shall be raised up with their own, same bodies, and none other,[6] although with different qualities, and these bodies shall be united again to their souls for ever.[7]

5 1 Cor 15.51-52; 1 Thess 4.17. **6** Job 19.26-27. **7** 1 Cor 15.42-43.

3. The bodies of the unjust shall, by the power of Christ, be raised to dishonour. The bodies of the just shall, by His Spirit, be raised to honour, and made conformable to *[transformed, remade, adapted to, made similar to]* His own glorious body.[8]

8 Acts 24.15; John 5.28-29; Phil 3.21.

32. The Last Judgement

1. God has appointed a day in which He will judge the world in righteousness, by Jesus Christ,[1] to Whom all power and judgement *[all judicial authority]* is given by the Father. In this day not only the apostate angels shall be judged,[2] but also all people who have lived

upon the earth. They shall appear before the tribunal *[judgement seat]* of Christ to give an account of their thoughts, words, and deeds, and to receive *[judgement]* according to what they have done when in the body, whether good or evil.[3]

1 Acts 17.31; John 5.22 & 27. 2 1 Cor 6.3; Jude 6.
3 2 Cor 5.10; Ecc 12.14; Matt 12.36; Rom 14.10-12; Matt 25.32-46.

2. The end *[purpose]* of God's appointing this day is for the manifestation of the glory of His mercy *[as seen]* in the eternal salvation of the elect, and also His justice, in the eternal damnation of the reprobate *[those disapproved and cast off]*, who are wicked and disobedient.[4] Then shall the righteous go into everlasting life and receive that fulness of joy and glory with everlasting reward in the presence of the Lord. But the wicked, who know not God and obey not the Gospel of Jesus Christ, shall be cast aside into everlasting torments,[5] and punished with everlasting destruction from the presence of the Lord and from the glory of His power.[6]

4 Rom 9.22-23. 5 Matt 25.21 & 34; 2 Tim 4.8.
6 Matt 25.46; Mark 9.48; 2 Thess 1.7-10.

3. As Christ would have us to be certainly persuaded that there will be a day of judgement, both to deter all men from sin[7] and to give greater consolation to the godly in their adversity,[8] so also He will have the date of that day kept unknown to men, that they may shake off all carnal security *[fleshly complacency]*, and always be watchful, because they know not at what hour the Lord will come.[9] Also, so that men *[believers]* may be affected in such a way that they ever say, 'Come Lord Jesus, come quickly!'[10] Amen.

7 2 Cor 5.10-11. 8 2 Thess 1.5-7. 9 Mark 13.35-37; Luke 12.35-40. 10 Rev 22.20.

Index to Subjects

This index refers readers to the commencing pages of chapters in which subjects are mainly dealt with. It is not a complete reference index. Such an index would be highly complex because of the repeated mention of most of these subjects throughout the *Confession.*

God's Rules for Holiness
Unlocking the Ten Commandments
139 pages, paperback, ISBN 978 1 870855 37 2

Taken at face value the Ten Commandments are binding on all people, and will guard the way to Heaven, so that evil will never spoil its glory and purity. But the Commandments are far greater than their surface meaning, as this book shows. They challenge us as Christians on a still wider range of sinful deeds and attitudes. They provide positive virtues as goals. And they give immense help for staying close to the Lord in our walk and worship.

The Commandments are vital for godly living and for greater blessing, but we need to enter into the panoramic view they provide for the standards and goals for redeemed people.

The Lord's Pattern for Prayer
118 pages, paperback, ISBN 978 1 870855 36 5

Subtitled – 'Studying the lessons and spiritual encouragements in the most famous of all prayers.' This volume is almost a manual on prayer, providing a real spur to the devotional life. The Lord's own plan and agenda for prayer – carefully amplified – takes us into the presence of the Father, to prove the privileges and power of God's promises to those who pray.

Chapters cover each petition in the Lord's Prayer. Here, too, are sections on remedies for problems in prayer, how to intercede for others, the reasons why God keeps us waiting for answers, and the nature of the prayer of faith.

Joshua's Conquest
Was it moral? What does it say to us today?
119 pages, paperback, ISBN 978 1 870855 46 4

Rooted in love for the Lord, Joshua was utterly faithful, wonderfully stable, and scrupulously obedient. The book of the Bible that bears his name is a magnificent anthology of events to challenge and inspire God's children in every age. This is a book for reading, rather than a commentary. Its aim is to bring out the spiritual message of *Joshua* for today, and also to explain some of the 'problem' portions and passages which evoke questions.

Worship in the Melting Pot
148 pages, paperback, ISBN 978 1 870855 33 4

'Worship is truly in the melting pot,' says the author. 'A new style of praise has swept into evangelical life shaking to the foundations traditional concepts and attitudes.' How should we react? Is it all just a matter of taste and age? Will churches be helped, or changed beyond recognition?

This book presents four essential principles which Jesus Christ laid down for worship, and by which every new idea must be judged. Here also is a fascinating view of how they worshipped in Bible times, including their rules for the use of instruments, and the question is answered – What does the Bible teach about the content and order of a service of worship today?

The Mutual Love of Christ and His People
An explanation of the *Song of Solomon* for personal devotions and Bible study groups
115 pages, paperback, ISBN 978 1 870855 40 2

The courtship of the *Song of Solomon* provides fascinating scenes and events designed to show the love of Christ for His redeemed people, and theirs for Him. Here, also, are lessons for Christians when they become cold or backslidden, showing the way to recover Christ's presence in their lives. Prophecies of Christ abound in the *Song*, together with views of the bride's destiny, as she prepares to cross the mountains into eternal glory, where the greatest wedding of all will take place.

This book begins with a brief overview of the reasons why the *Song* should be seen as allegorical – the viewpoint held throughout church history by the overwhelming majority of preachers and commentators. Then, in verse-by-verse mode, but designed for continuous devotional reading, the symbols are explained and applied.

Physicians of Souls
The Gospel Ministry
285 pages, paperback, ISBN 978 1 870855 34 1

'Compelling, convicting, persuasive preaching, revealing God's mercy and redemption to dying souls, is seldom heard today. The noblest art ever granted to our fallen human race has almost disappeared.'

Even where the free offer of the Gospel is treasured in principle, regular evangelistic preaching has become a rarity, contends the author. These pages tackle the inhibitions, theological and practical, and provide powerful encouragement for physicians of souls to preach the Gospel. A vital anatomy or order of conversion is supplied with advice for counselling seekers.

The author shows how passages for evangelistic persuasion may be selected and prepared. He also challenges modern church growth techniques, showing the superiority of direct proclamation. These and other key topics make up a complete guide to soul-winning.

Not Like Any Other Book

161 pages, paperback, ISBN 978 1 870855 43 3

Faulty Bible interpretation lies at the root of every major mistake and 'ism' assailing churches today, and countless Christians are asking for the old, traditional and proven way of handling the Bible to be spelled out plainly.

A new approach to interpretation has also gripped many evangelical seminaries and Bible colleges, an approach based on the ideas of unbelieving critics, stripping the Bible of God's message, and leaving pastors impoverished in their preaching. This book reveals what is happening, providing many brief examples of right and wrong interpretation. The author shows that the Bible includes its own rules of interpretation, and every believer should know what these are.

Heritage of Evidence

127 pages, illustrated, paperback, ISBN 978 1 870855 39 6

In today's atheistic climate most people have no idea how much powerful evidence exists for the literal accuracy and authenticity of the biblical record. The British Museum holds a huge number of major discoveries that provide direct corroboration and background confirmation for an immense sweep of Bible history. This survey of Bible-authenticating exhibits has been designed as a guide for visitors, and also to give pleasure and interest to readers unable to tour the galleries. It will also be most suitable for people who need to see the accuracy and inspiration of the Bible.

Almost every item viewed on the tour receives a full colour photograph. Room plans are provided for every gallery visited showing the precise location of artefacts, and time-charts relate the items to contemporary kings and prophets. The book is enriched by pictures and descriptions of famous 'proofs' in other museums.

Men of Purpose

157 pages, illustrated, paperback, ISBN 978 1 870855 41 9

This book brings into one illustrated volume eleven great lives, all with an experience of personal conversion to God. Composer Mendelssohn, food industrialist Henry Heinz, novelist Daniel Defoe, and some of the most celebrated scientists of all time, are among the examples of leading people whose lives were changed by a sight of real Christianity. Also very suitable as a gift to unconverted friends, and to enrich sermons and Bible class messages.

www.wakemantrust.org